Who Cares

Help for Those Caring for Seriously
Ill Loved Ones at Home

Joan Wilson-Jones

BALBOA.
PRESS

A DIVISION OF HAY HOUSE

Balboa Press books may be ordered through booksellers or by contacting:

Balboa Press
A Division of Hay House
1663 Liberty Drive
Bloomington, IN 47403
www.balboapress.com.au
1 (877) 407-4847

Print information available on the last page.

ISBN: 978-1-4525-2826-7 (sc)
ISBN: 978-1-4525-2827-4 (e)

Balboa Press rev. date: 04/15/2015

Dedicated to Philip and Helen with love

Some will step out of the darkness while others wait for the light to shine in its own good time. For me, I rode home. Secure on the broad back of my giant Clydesdale I returned to welcome a new day and to step into the next important phase of this thing we call life

We were nearly put off by the rain. In fact we'd conceded defeat on the Friday and gone to the movies instead. Saturday greeted us again with showers but this time we thought 'what the hell' and loaded the two mares onto the float and set off anyway. We were well rewarded as the weather held and the riding was exhilarating and energising. By Sunday, we are beyond second thoughts and just determined to ride.

Parts of the gentle, undulating bridle paths are soggy from all the rain. As we approach a lookout, I allow Mischief to find her own pace and space. We rest for a few minutes, horse and rider gazing transfixed at the sweeping vista before us. There are rolling hills, with the sharp rise of mountains in the distance. Beyond them I know lies the ocean, and I throw my head back and breathe.

So much has brought me to here. In this moment, as I gaze contentedly towards the horizon, I am filled with emotional flashbacks as my psyche takes time to connect with this new place and new time. I remind myself I live here now; that still seems surreal in itself. I remind myself I have time to ride—whole day rides, sweet gentle rides, fast daring rides—time to do and time to be. That feels odd, quite alien, and in some unexplainable way, almost uncomfortable. Is it guilt? Do I feel unworthy, undeserving of this time, this freedom? Or maybe it is just unfamiliarity. Maybe I just need time for me to adjust and accept.

When we dare to dream, we open up so many possibilities, and when dreams come to pass, it can be difficult to accept their unfolding. I call it 'dream shock'. It's a type of culture shock, where your life has evolved into a whole new experience, but that experience is foreign and it doesn't fit well. Our neural pathways haven't adjusted to see this as 'normal' and the 'abnormality' can feel uncomfortable (even when it's good). I remind myself that, just like when we drop ourselves into a new country, when we suddenly put ourselves into a whole new life, it takes time to adjust, understand, accept and enjoy.

The rest over, we head through the lookout and out towards Kin Kin. The view continues to grab my attention. I watch the gentle movement of the horse in front of me. I engage in easy, idle conversation with the other rider. I act and interact as if I am coping with this just fine, but inside my heart is bursting and my spirit is soaring because this IS me and I AM here. This is real and this is wonderful and I am finally in a space where I can explore the story that brought me to this place.

Here is one very big and significant chapter in that story.

Enjoy—really enjoy—life and all it offers

As we know, some years are bigger than others, and 2002, it turned out, was to be a very big year for Philip and me. We had no idea when it started (as is often the case) that with the turning of the calendar, our lives were being launched in a whole new direction. Ahead of us lay some rather enormous obstacles and a range of inspiring triumphs. It was a journey that would stretch us almost to breaking point while providing an unprecedented opportunity for growth and learning. Looking back, I'm interested to note that I have no recollection of how we saw this momentous year in. Did we celebrate? Did we stay up until midnight and herald the year feeling full of optimism and hope? I don't know. The transition from 2001 to 2002 is just a blur now.

It started back in late 2001. Our relationship had transcended awkward infancy and survived consolidation, and even for two people as cautious and independent as Philip and I, having celebrated a decade as a couple, it seemed fitting that we might now consider the giant step of moving in together. We'd been deep in discussions, with lots of planning, projecting, surmising and even some forays into property searches. We were undecided about the location and unsure about the timeframes. However, we both agreed that we'd like some space (acreage) to enable us to fulfil my lifelong dream of having a 'little farm'.

In November 2001, we attended a wedding in the Samford Valley (in Queensland, just north of Brisbane). Both the ceremony and the reception were held at a popular local restaurant. Perched high atop a hill, the grounds offered amazing views of the valley. While the wedding party had the mandatory series of photos taken, guests were left to their own devices with celebratory champagne and an array of delicious finger food. It was a warm night, and the sun lingered in the sky, reluctant to leave for the day and Philip and I stood absorbing the view.

'Wouldn't it be great to live out here?' I said.

'It's infinitely possible,' he replied.

The new year saw us looking more determinedly at properties. We decided to do a reconnaissance, mainly to establish property values and determine whether the pipe dream could be transformed into reality. I was heading off to America in May for two months to fulfil a contract with California State University, and preparations for that were well underway. Combined with my very busy Australia-based work schedule, there wasn't much time for house hunting, let alone the effort required to sell two houses and buy one should we find something we liked.

So we were trawling the net, checking prices and areas, getting a sense of what land size we wanted and basically just getting a feel for what was around. Our plan was to look more determinedly when I returned from America in July. After all, buying a house on the verge of a two month absence really wasn't a very clever move, was it?

In my searching, I came across a house that intrigued me. It really didn't suit, it was too far out of the village and it was almost new (so there were no gardens or infrastructure in place at all). This meant that our top two, non-negotiable requirements weren't being met by this property, but it looked amazing in the photographs and the video walk-through tour really had me fascinated. I showed Philip and we both agreed it wasn't what we wanted, but we were both inspired to have a look. The work of a well-known Sunshine Coast architect, the house ticked all our eco boxes and offered a floor plan that was gloriously creative and oozing originality.

We made time a few days later to go and have a look. I had business meetings scheduled and needed to be in the city by late morning, so it was really just a quick look—something to soothe our curiosity. While we were out in the valley, I agreed to let the agent show us a couple of other properties. It couldn't hurt to see some of the places I'd been exploring on the net in real life and that way we could start to better understand how to interpret descriptions and photographs (start learning 'real estate sales speak' if you like). We saw the expedition as the next step in our research. We had no intention of buying anything; we were both clearly agreed on that. This is always a dangerous position.

I knew the minute my foot touched the land that we were going to buy it. The gate was locked and the key the agent had with him refused to work (despite us all having a go). Ironically, that same key worked perfectly for years after. Undeterred, we climbed through the fence. I was dressed for business meetings, but an uncooperative key, a fitted skirt and a pair of flimsy shoes weren't stopping me from seeing this property. I delicately picked my way through the wire strands, and it was my right foot that first touched what was to be our new home. A massive surge of energy bolted from my toes to top of my head. My body tingled and a warm glow overtook me. I needed to look no further (though of course we did).

The property captivated both of us from the start. We wove our way through stones and mud to the front door. I heard the sound of running water and immediately saw the source of it as the agent opened the double front doors. There to greet us was an indoor pond with a fountain. You accessed the house via a timber bridge that spanned the water. It just got better.

When we'd decided to move onto acreage, I'd imagined a quaint country farmhouse, complete with verandah and rocking chair. This house was as far from this picture as you could possibly imagine.

Our new home was gloriously unusual, wonderfully eco-friendly and incredibly serene, but 'quaint country farmhouse' it wasn't. Perched on five acres of rock, shale and mud, despite having being occupied for five months, the house had the appearance of a building site. Others might look and see hours of back-breaking work, paddocks and yards to establish, grass to encourage, a forest of weeds to clear, in fact everywhere you looked it just screamed 'work, work, work', but my heart sang as I envisioned what it could become.

'What if we put some paddocks down there?' I was to say once we'd moved in. 'We'd be able to see the animals from the deck.'

'Deck?' questioned Philip. 'What deck?

'Oh, what if we put a deck out there? It would allow us to see the paddocks. 'There was a multitude of 'what if' statements. I heard Philip lament to friends over dinner one night, 'Every other sentence she mutters starts with 'what if'. Clearly, we're living at 'What If Farm'.' The name stuck.

We'd left home determined not to buy anything. Within a couple of hours we were making an offer, and the following morning we signed the deal. So here we were, with three houses and a heap of unplanned debt, and I was about to leave for a two month stint in America. Ordinarily I would have been worried, but I was too elated to be even the slightest bit concerned. It would sort itself out, I knew it would. And of course, it did.

My house sold within 24 hours of listing it, Philip's a few weeks later. We launched ourselves into the task of moving two houses and two businesses. It turned out to be a 17 hour epic event, but before the removal truck had left the driveway we'd already popped the champagne and were toasting our new life. I remember being wildly happy and optimistic in that moment. I remember thinking it was all coming together. I remember a blissful sense of delirium. As we sat exhausted, surrounded by a maze of boxes and contentedly sipping champagne, there was no hint of what was to come.

I look back on that moment now and I hope I enjoyed it enough. I hope I allowed myself to be truly engaged. And as I reflect on that evening, the Buddhist mantra of 'this too shall pass' echoes in my head. And it did.

Take opportunities as they arise (and chase after them if they don't)

I'd never heard of Fresno, California until it was confirmed I was going there. Once the contract had been signed, I looked it up only to find it was listed as the 'crime capital of America'. Well, at least it should be interesting, I thought.

The lead up to getting to Fresno had in itself been interesting. Sue-Ellen (a friend and business partner) and I had been keen to be part of the California State (CalState) University's *Summer Arts* program since we'd first heard about it the year before.

Two independent business consultants, we had teamed up to create a third, combined business in 2000. We were both committed to the joint business venture and continually on the lookout for interesting projects we could become involved in. Having heard about *Summer Arts*, we were determined to go. Neither of us considered it to be a major obstacle that the *Summer Arts* activities (a series of creative master classes offered over the summer break for the cream of CalState's arts students) bore no relation to anything we did professionally. We were intrigued and excited by what we'd heard and we really wanted to be part of it. We set about sending ideas and proposals, all of which were politely declined. Sue-Ellen and I are not women to be easily deterred, and we saw each rejection as an opportunity to come up with another idea.

When we originally established our professional partnership, Sue-Ellen and I had celebrated by going hot air ballooning. As the year 2001 started to come to a close, we pondered what we could do to mark our successful first year of operations.

'If we were Indian, we'd get our horoscopes done,' I mused as I poured us both another coffee.

'Ummm, interesting you should say that,' she responded, reaching for the milk. 'Because just the other day, somebody gave me the business card of an astrologer and said he's really good. I can't remember where I put it, but if I can find it when I get home, what about we take that as a sign and we'll go and get our charts done?'

It sounded like a plan. We finished our coffee and she headed home.

At that time, Sue-Ellen lived about 20 minutes drive from me. Twenty-five minutes after she'd left my place my phone rang. 'I don't believe it,' she declared. 'It's here in the middle of my desk, and I know for a fact I didn't put it there!'

She didn't need to tell me what 'it' was. We booked sequential appointments, made a pact not to let on to the astrologer that we knew each other, and identified the coffee shop where we'd meet afterwards for the debrief.

My appointment was first. For an hour, he mostly talked about what had already happened to me. Admittedly, he was pretty accurate, but I did wonder why someone would pay someone else to tell them when they'd had their appendix out (a fact that I was already very familiar with). I was starting to get a bit disgruntled when it got interesting.

'You're off to the States,' he said.

'When?' I enquired excitedly.

'Next year. It's work—the contract will come through; you've been working on it for a while. It's going to happen.'

The reading over, I stood up to leave. As part of the goodbyes he said 'and have a good holiday overseas.'

I was standing at the door of his reading room and I turned to him and responded, 'What? I'm not going overseas for a holiday.'

'Yes you are,' he said. 'It's all booked and paid for. You leave soon.'

I searched my brain for information about an upcoming overseas holiday. Clearly one of us was going mad. Unable to access any information to support his statement, I concluded that it must be he. 'No I'm not,' I insisted.

'Joan, where are you going in January?'

'New Zealand, to walk the Milford Track.'

'Yes' he replied, 'and last time I looked, New Zealand was overseas. Have a great time.'

Well of course it is, I pondered to myself, wondering how I could have forgotten that. He walked out with me and just as we got to the front door the bell chimed, announcing the arrival of

Sue-Ellen. Now Sue-Ellen really is an actor and I'm not too bad at bluffing (except when I'm playing poker, apparently) and we both agreed later that our cursory 'hellos' as we passed in the hallway were sufficiently vague as to suggest we were strangers. Our astrologer, however, was not to be fooled.

I headed to the coffee shop and immersed myself in a book and a soy latte. Some 80 minutes later Sue-Ellen arrived, grinning from ear to ear. 'We've been sprung,' she announced.

Towards the end of her reading our star gazer had asked her, 'So how well do you know the woman who was just here?'

'I don't,' she insisted, with all the confidence of someone who's read the script and taken on the character.

'The woman in the hallway when you arrived, you don't know her?'

'No.'

'You're sure?'

'Yes.'

'Well that's very interesting,' he mused. 'Never before have I met someone who runs a business with someone who they've never met. You see, there is a strong alignment here; you're both going to America to work together. Oh, but you're not going to New Zealand. You're sure you don't know her?'

After our coffee, Sue-Ellen returned to her office and sent an email to the director of the *Summer Arts* program saying that we'd just seen an astrologer who'd said we were coming over to work and so they might want to send the contracts (an approach that until now hadn't really featured in our thinking). The contracts arrived shortly thereafter, and in June 2002 we became part of the *Summer Arts* team.

Despite being billed as the crime capital of America, I found Fresno to be quite charming. The university campus is well positioned, gloriously close to Yosemite National Park, a place that was to become very dear to me, and it quickly became evident that we were set for an amazing time. We were housed in student accommodation which had the wonderful convenience of a well-operating air conditioning system. This was a feature we very much appreciated as the desert temperatures frequently went over the 100 degree Fahrenheit mark.

Sue-Ellen and I took to our roles as co-ordinators of cross genre interaction like the proverbial ducks to water. Our days were spent encouraging students to look beyond their particular discipline. We worked with them to help them to collaborate and combine their talents in ways that enhanced the learning of everybody and our evenings were spent attending functions and concerts. It was an idyllic, inspiring time, and we got paid for it!

Philip had stayed at the farm to finish the unpacking and, unbeknownst to me, to build a deck. (We'd agreed on the plans before I left, but I hadn't imagined it would be completed by the time I got home.) It seemed odd to be away just when our dream was just starting to unfold, but the contract in America was so energising and exciting that we'd both declared it was worth it.

'And anyway,' declared Philip during one of our discussions, 'we'll have our whole lives together once you get home.'

Be aware that there is no right way to hear bad news

We were about two weeks into the four week *Summer Arts* contract. We'd settled into a rhythm of life on campus and were feeling like an integral part of the team. In short, the whole experience was going very well. On one particular evening, having just returned from yet another amazing student performance, I took a stroll across the campus to make my evening phone call home. It was a balmy evening, the moon, not quite full, hovered in the clear sky, surrounded by endless shining stars. I was feeling relaxed and content. I watched intrigued from my position in the only campus phone box as a fox sauntered across the lawn. Said fox seemed very at home, sniffing the grass and wandering slowly around. I could hear the phone ringing at the other end and enjoyed having a focus for my gaze as I waited for Philip to answer. He sounded tired when he got to the phone.

'I'm sorry', I said, 'did I stuff up the time difference?'

'No, you're fine. I'm just a bit tired.'

I knew it was something more. I could tell from his voice. He knew I knew; he realised he needed to explain.

'I need to tell you something.' His voice was soft, and I could hear he was trying to hide fear. 'I haven't been well, I'm been to the doctor, I'm taking these antibiotics and they're really knocking me around.'

'What's the problem?' Nothing felt right. Even across the geographic distance that was between us I was picking up signals.

'They're not sure—well the doctor thinks it's probably an infection, so they've given me antibiotics.' The rest of the conversation revealed that Philip's symptoms had been going on for some time. He was having trouble urinating and it was getting worse. The doctor, without doing blood or urine tests, had proclaimed that he was too young for it to be serious and had prescribed antibiotics.

'See another doctor,' I encouraged.

'We'll see how this goes,' he replied.

When I hung up, my hand was shaking and I stayed in the phone box for some minutes just watching the fox that was standing statue-like, watching me. He didn't move, even when I finally left the phone box. I walked around him and his eyes followed my movement. I walked for over an hour before I went back to the unit I was sharing with Sue-Ellen. I knew from Philip's voice that he was worried and I intuitively knew that something was not good. Alarm bells were sounding in my head. It was three days before I could recount the conversation to Sue-Ellen. On a rational level I knew that panic was premature as we had no idea what was happening, but I also felt strongly that whatever it was, it was serious. When the full story of Philip's health was revealed some months later, I remembered the conversation with the astrologer and noted that Philip had never been mentioned (past, present or future). Suddenly, that seemed odd and uncomfortable.

As the days and weeks passed, Philip's voice became more and more tired. The first round of antibiotics had done nothing to relieve the original symptoms, so the general practitioner (or GP) prescribed another round, ramping up the potency and as a result further sapping Philip's energy. Philip confessed to me that some days he couldn't get out of bed at all.

My worry radar was beeping loudly and I continued to suggest strongly that it might be time to see another doctor. After all, second opinions can't hurt and there had still been no tests taken, so the drugs were being prescribed without any supporting pathology or information. Philip held firm in his loyalty to the doctor who had been his family GP for some years.

I had plans to stay on in California at the conclusion of the work contract, but my concern for Philip's health was ringing such alarm bells that I kept insisting that I come home as soon as the work commitment finished.

Philip was equally emphatic that I stay.

'I'll be fine,' he insisted. 'I'm sure it's just an infection and it's just taking a while to clear up. You watch, by the time you get home, I'll be well again.'

Philip's health was a long way from improved by the time I got home. When he met me at the airport he was pale and drawn. He had clearly lost weight, his eyes were dull and his hands fidgety. He did his best to put on a brave face, asking about the trip, but frequently drifting off when I tried to answer. His focus seemed disjointed.

He was still seeing the original GP, the antibiotics were still ongoing, the original symptoms were unresolved and his energy levels were almost non-existent. Still no tests of any nature had been undertaken.

I could see him going downhill, yet any suggestion for him to see another doctor just continued to fall on deaf ears. Philip was scared and his fear was fuelling his capacity to hold firm on a swirling river of denial. The sails were set and the boat was on course and nothing I said made any difference, so I shut up.

At that time, Philip's work situation was, to say the least, precarious. He had held an elected position in the union movement for many years, but a change of alliance on his part had seen that career end in an election disappointment. He had spent the next few years back at university, funding his study through a home handyman business he started. (If Philip hadn't grown up to be a negotiator, I think he would have relished life as a builder.) On graduating with an almost perfect grade point average, he had started contract work doing mediations, negotiations and a range of workshops.

The work was sporadic and he was finding it hard to make a reasonable living. As I was fully booked with work it wasn't too much of an issue, and with the new property to get sorted, having Philip and his tool box around was quite a blessing. That he was now in a position of not being able to get out of bed most days wasn't really helping to get things done. He'd lament endlessly to me how much he wanted to get into the tasks. There were fences to be constructed, barns to build, and a chicken coop was high on the list. The list languished as Philip battled fatigue and the emotional malaise that swept in opportunistically on the back of his ill health.

Finally, even Philip could take no more, and on the urging of a friend, he booked an appointment with a new doctor recommended by her. A series of tests were immediately organised and the results clearly disputed any infection. A physical examination revealed a massively oversized, misshapen and hardened prostate, and in less than the time it took for Philip to get dressed following the examination, the doctor had booked an appointment with a specialist urologist. The PSA (prostate specific antigen) was in double figures, which in itself was reason for concern, but it was the physical examination that really had the medico hopping.

'Here's your appointment, Philip,' she said sternly. 'It's the earliest one I could get. Whatever you have to cancel to get to it, cancel it. This is more important. Am I making myself clear?'

Philip came home in shock. 'She's really worried,' he proclaimed and at that point I think I started to realise that we might have just been given two tickets on the world's scariest roller coaster. The urologist appointment was for 9th September 2002, Philip's 49th birthday.

We both decided that this new GP was one we wanted on our team. That the original GP had been prepared to diagnose and prescribe without so much as a single test resulted in his dismissal (somewhat late, but I wasn't on the hiring and firing team at this stage). It then came out that Philip had seen the same doctor some two years earlier with the same symptoms and, getting no results then, had finally given up and just gotten on with things. When I heard this, I was livid.

'What!' I screamed. 'Why didn't you get a second opinion then? You've been living with this for two years—bloody hell!' Then I went quiet, because I felt the terror surge from him.

'I got the answer I wanted,' he whispered. 'He sent me away and said I was too young for it to be cancer.'

It's hard not to speculate. If that original doctor had ordered some tests back then and followed up with treatment, would the outcome have been different? Prostate cancer can be very treatable if caught early. Would that early visit have been early enough? I am still plagued by questions for which I will never have any answers.

Having made the shift to the new GP, Philip then contacted the original doctor and asked him to transfer his records. He received a rather snappy note back stating that while it was his decision who he saw for his medical treatment, did he really trust 'a girl' (the new doctor was female) with his health care? I was angry before, but now I was speechless. Breathe, I repeated to myself in my morning meditations. Breathe and move on.

Don't always rely on doctors—
but DO rely on friends

Ann and George had arrived from England! We'd first met Ann
and George over breakfast in Marrakesh. I am forever amazed
at the simple ways that incredible people enter your life. Is there
a stage manager hovering up in the universe saying, 'enter stage
right now'? I have a zillion stories of chance interactions that
proved both life changing and life enhancing. There have been
strangers who have emerged from crowds and with single word
introductions stayed in my life for years, fleeting angels who
have gotten me out of many a fix and wondrous beings who have
brought untold joy to my experience here at Earth school.

One misty morning in Marrakesh, via the conduit of orange
juice, Ann and George drifted into our lives. They were scripted
for big parts. They remain a significant part of my existence.
None of us could have guessed where a simple question would
lead us. If we had, would Ann have had the courage to ask it and
would I have taken the time to answer? Who knows? The stage
manager had directed, the play continued, and the cast was
getting into position.

'Is that real orange juice?' someone enquired in a strong
Yorkshire accent.

'Yes,' I replied and, boom, a friendship was born. This friendship
was to embrace adventure and excitement. It grew aloft camels,

deepened in deserts, was fed by waterside fish sellers, embraced celebrations, participated in parties and held fast through the most difficult of times. It amazes me how such an inane conversation can lead to such an invaluable connection. I've never thought of orange juice in the same way since that brief exchange on that rooftop.

Now, we were sharing breakfast again, on the deck at What If Farm, such a long way from a rooftop in Marrakesh. Freshly squeezed orange juice once again featured on the menu, except this time the conversation was guarded, and just a little tense. In a few hours, Philip had an appointment with the specialist urologist and he was trying desperately to ignore the fact. George tried hard to broach the subject. 'How are you, Philip?' he asked.

'Shall I make more coffee?' Philip responded. The conversation moved on and the dreaded elephant settled into the corner of the room, but it was far from unnoticed. Philip's response told us all that he didn't want to talk about it. We respected his wishes and I felt an ache as the shrivelling in my soul inched inwards a little bit more.

We arrived early at the urologist's surgery. 'Oh,' said the receptionist, 'if I'd realised it was your birthday, I would have made a cake.'

We sat stony-faced in the waiting room. Why are doctors' waiting rooms always littered with old magazines? I managed to find one with a four page spread of a celebrity wedding. The next magazine I picked up announced the impending divorce of the same couple. The ironic twist of fate wasn't lost on me. Gains and losses, isn't that what life is all about? We waited impatiently and in silence.

Philip's name was finally called. We both got up. 'No, just Philip,' stated the stern-faced doctor.

We both knew that this visit had the potential to hold difficult news.

'Can't Joan come in too?' Philip asked.

'What, are you some kind of wuss or something?' was the reply.

I stood there stunned. I couldn't believe what I'd just heard.

'She can come in if you want her to,' conceded the doctor, somewhat reluctantly.

I looked around his consulting rooms. Patient files (clearly displaying names, addresses and dates of birth) littered his desk. Clearly, confidentiality wasn't a high priority for him. I wondered if anybody had ever sat in this chair and seen a friend's file or maybe a favourite uncle's sitting on the desk and learnt that someone close to them had reason to see this doctor.

He asked Philip a few questions; he checked the medical reports. He asked what the first GP said. Philip tried to respond with information from the second GP. The urologist ignored him and repeated the original question. I breathed deeply and my lungs were invaded by the bitter stench of dismissal. The boys were sticking together, it seemed. In any event, whether there was a gender bias or not, he stuck with the first doctor.

'I don't think you've given the antibiotics a good enough chance,' he smiled and I felt sickened. 'So I'm going to suggest we try another course.'

I was stunned, and even more so when Philip, the rebel of all rebels, the quintessential arguer, the man who had made his living refuting points and disagreeing with people, compliantly murmured, 'ok.'

I couldn't wait to leave the surgery. I felt myself preparing to explode but I knew I couldn't, because it was fear driving Philip. I wanted to shake him and I wanted to throw all the files littering the office at the doctor and I wanted to scream and I wanted to hit something and I wanted to collapse and I wanted someone to wake me up and tell me it was all a dream but instead, I followed Philip out of the room and we were halfway home before I found my voice to speak.

'Why?' was all I could manage.

'Because I'm too tired to fight,' was his reply.

To be honest, I can't remember how we celebrated that birthday. I'm sure we all did our best. Was there cake? There must have been. Maybe we went out for dinner. Who would know? Everything went blurry when Philip said 'ok', and no clarity about that day has yet returned. Of course, the story continues and much was yet to happen, but the details of Philip's 49th birthday are lost in the emotional muck of dread and the sludge of disbelief that in the lottery of doctors we'd drawn three times and got two duds!

Relish the good times

There was going to be a wedding! Well, a wedding of sorts. When we purchased the property, Philip announced that it was important to him that we made a public commitment. He'd often mentioned getting married, but I was very gun shy when it came to anything legal. I'd been married at the age of 17 and still carried the emotional and psychological scars, to say nothing of the memories of the financial difficulties I had experienced post-divorce. Marriage and I weren't great playmates. That said, I love a good party, so a compromise was quickly made.

We decided on a pagan hand fasting. The idea appealed to me. It is an ancient ritual whereby a couple commit for one year and one day. Each year the vows are either re-taken or the couple separate. I liked the concept of 'for as long as we're happy'. Maybe divorce had left me cynical, but it seemed to me that 'forever' is a bloody long time and none of us know what the future holds. The commitment ceremony plans were fitted in as Philip's energy levels allowed. His health was clearly going backwards, though whether that was because of the antibiotics or the condition that they were supposed to be combatting was unclear.

We set the date for the September full moon (which had kindly accommodated us by appearing on a Saturday night). Normally new starts would be made on a new moon, but both Philip and I had a strong attachment to the full moon and we both felt strongly that with a giant cheese ball as a witness, we had to stand a better chance.

A true believer in 'signs', I constantly scanned the minute details of each day for messages of hope that might serve to help me stay focused. On the night of our ceremony we received what I can only call a blast of cosmic encouragement that still has even the most hardened sceptics talking.

In the lead up to the commitment ceremony, a friend presented me with a bag of floating candles. She was to be overseas when the event happened, and on presenting me with her gift had said, 'I don't care where you put these, but I want them to be part of the evening so that, through them, I am with you.'

I showed Philip and candles and shared the message. 'Ummm', he replied. 'Well, they aren't going in the spa (as part of the new deck construction Philip had included a full-sized therapeutic spa) and they aren't going in the indoor pond, because the melting wax might muck up the drainage, but other than that, I'm happy with wherever you decide to put them.' It didn't leave me many options really, so I decided on the only spot left—the dam at the bottom of the paddock.

The deck (where the ceremony was to be held) afforded a great view of the dam, so all in all, the only option didn't seem like a bad option.

As the sun set on the evening of the celebrations, the candles were carefully lit and set free on the dam. A gentle breeze took control and herded every last candle into a bunch and gathered them in a haphazard group against one of the side walls. Despite a breeze that was sufficient to move them all, not one of them lost its flame.

As guests arrived, said candles now appeared as a small blob flickering in the distance. This was not quite the effect I'd hoped for; I'd imagined them dotted randomly across the surface area of the dam. However, they were there, and they were lit and my promise to my friend had been honoured.

I had organised a high priestess of a local Wicca coven to officiate. Philip and I both come from strongly Christian families and we'd tossed up on this decision a lot, as we naturally didn't want to offend or upset anyone. In the end, this felt right for us. I researched the origins of the hand fasting ceremony, and the information I'd been able to find confirmed our decision that it was a highly meaningful ceremony for us. Philip wrote a moving speech which he delivered before the ceremony started. He urged people to not take offence if the proceedings differed from their beliefs, and emphasised that our decision to go with this approach was not meant to upset in any way.

The high priestess then stepped forward and 'cast the magic circle'. At this moment, a truly amazing thing happened. The candles on the dam all repositioned themselves to form a massive and perfect circle (despite the still persistent breeze). I heard people gasp and comment. The candle circle remained for the entire ceremony. At the conclusion, when the magic circle was reopened, the candles all returned to their congregated gathering at the edge of the dam. The moon glowed down on us in all her glory and for one whole evening, the world was safe and we celebrated and laughed.

We had written our own ceremony and I was aware that it was serious and somewhat heavy, so to lighten the mood, when the circle was opened we led the way in a massive dance. Guests joined the family, and hand in hand, we wove our way all through the house and around the grounds. The haunting sounds of the Celtic harp quickly merged with the laughter and our home was filled with joy and friendship as over 300 feet danced through every room. As I write this I am transported back to that moment, the music, the night air, the enormous full moon and the laughter and I am reminded that even in the midst of fear and terror, there is wonder and unadulterated joy. Memories aren't separated by time—rather, they walk with us side by side in every moment that we acknowledge them and every time we revisit them.

A few months and many medical test results later, Philip presented me with an eternity ring (made to match my wedding ring) saying, 'I know you're supposed to wait a year before you get this, but we don't know if we have a year and anyway, I figure it's ok, because it took me an eternity to find you.'

There are no rules in life. There are merely guidelines that we can massage and imbue with meanings and messages direct from our hearts.

Fight for your rights (and take help when it's offered)

More antibiotics and more debilitating tiredness, and then we returned to the urologist to report that Philip's symptoms were just getting worse. Our concerns were again dismissed with summations of 'you're too young for anything serious.'

Which medical book did that come out of, I asked myself? When has cancer ever been a respecter of age?

Finally Philip's fight returned and I saw again the man I had seen take on employers in the Industrial Relations Commission, the fighter for justice that I had witnessed at union rallies and the warrior of determination I had heard across radio waves and television broadcasts. On this second visit to the urologist Philip stood up, leant over the desk and said firmly but quietly, 'Either schedule a biopsy or I'll get an appointment with another doctor.'

The specialist went down fighting. 'If you insist,' he snarled, 'but it's an invasive procedure and I don't think you need it.'

'We'll see,' said Philip. 'I'll get the details from your receptionist. See you at the hospital.' With that he stood upright, grabbed my hand and calmly walked out. Ah, thought I, from the fog of all those drugs, a man I recognise has just returned.

The biopsies were duly completed. I picked Philip up from the hospital afterwards and he was pale and shaking. He was laid up for a good three days, in significant pain, and feeling (in his words) like a train had run over him.

It was on a Friday that he dragged himself out of bed to attend a meeting he had scheduled as part of his part-time role on the staff of local state politician Geoff Wilson. Federal politician Wayne Swann was also scheduled to be at that meeting and Wayne had arrived early that day. He greeted Philip warmly and, as we do, enquired automatically about Philip's health.

As it happens, Philip had just got off the phone from the urologist who was reporting in with the biopsy results. 'This is the call I hoped I wouldn't have to make,' the doctor had said. 'It's cancer—looks advanced. I took five biopsies and they are all positive. It appears the gland is completely consumed. I need to see you as soon as you can get here.' And that's how Philip was told he had an invasive, aggressive, Grade 5 cancer.

When Wayne asked the automatic question, 'How are you, Philip?' he wouldn't have expected the reply.

'It seems I have cancer. Doesn't sound too good from what the specialist just said—prostate. Whole thing's shot, from the sounds of it.'

Wayne immediately cancelled the meeting and spent the next two hours with Philip, going through options and information. It was a much needed 'boy's talk', I suspect. When Philip phoned me with the biopsy results, his response to my saying, 'I'll come and get you' was 'No, you're fine; I'm going to chat to Wayne and then I'll come home'.

I remember phoning my daughters, I remember phoning a couple of close friends, I remember crying the first of many tears (I'd been dry-eyed but scared up until now) and I remember trying to be in control when Philip got home. We had a sombre evening. His children came over and he rang and spoke to his mum. We still had no idea what we were dealing with, but we sensed that it had the potential to be majorly challenging. The following day, my daughters visited and by the following week we were launched into an exhausting raft of what felt like endless tests and results.

The journey, as they say, had truly begun.

*Expect to be angry and to not cope as
well as you may think you should*

Well, if we thought life was driven by medical stuff before the diagnosis, once the biopsy results were in, our whole existence turned upside down. A barrage of scans and tests were ordered as we now needed to establish how widespread the cancer was.

If still contained to the prostate, the prognosis was good. Surgery would be a viable option and, if successful, the surgeon's knife could well cut this intruder completely from our lives.

Our days were full of waiting rooms, more of those out of date magazines and lots of serious faces. Each test came back with worse news than the one before. It was hard for us to stay resolved and focused. Suddenly a whole new array of 'what if' questions filled our day. But rather than the excitement of 'what if we built a paddock?', now we were facing 'what if this is really bad?' We never actually said the dreaded 'T' word. It was hard enough to say 'cancer' and it was to be a long time before either of us could muster the courage to even think the word 'terminal'.

It was hard to imagine that just a few short months earlier we had moved to the farm full of hope and optimism. Philip had been full of confidence that he would successfully get his own consultancy business off the ground and, with both of us to share expenses, it had seemed realistic that I could pull back my workload to something resembling part-time. This would give me time to run the farm and hopefully do some writing (a dream I had long held but hadn't yet managed to realise). Suddenly, that dream was yanked out from under us.

Philip had no private health insurance and, with the long waits in the public system, we opted to go private and pay. That we'd just bought a new property, with all the associated costs of that move, meant there was already some financial pressure on us, and the medical tests just increased that worry.

It's only now as I look back that I realise how angry I was and how totally ripped off I felt. Instead of enjoying the planned idyllic, bohemian lifestyle that I had so long dreamed about and which had been tantalisingly, yet briefly, waved in front of my face, here I was thrust into the role of primary bread winner, sole bill payer and, with Philip's health invariably compromised due to the constant tests and psychological impact of the results, I was also doing the lion's share of the property maintenance.

And I was scared—terrifyingly, nightmarishly, paralysingly scared.

I scoured the book shops, libraries and websites looking for insights into how to get through this. I needed some help dealing with my fears about how to be the primary support person, how to manage the demons that haunted me, how to regain some balance in my life and how to cope on a minute by minute basis. Sadly, I found very little.

I did find some great books written by doctors and complementary therapists, and wonderful insightful works written by cancer survivors. I even found some informative stuff written by the friends and carers of those who didn't survive the cancer, but I struggled to find what felt to me like the truth about being the carer.

The medical tomes offered advice (some of which felt like platitudes) and in stories written by cancer survivors, the carer was portrayed as a saint who did nothing wrong and was always serene and pleasant. The books written by the carers themselves generally focused on the patient's story rather than the carer.

I desperately wanted to talk to someone who'd been through it. I wanted to know if other carers woke up in the middle of night in a sweat of fear, fuelled by panic and resentment (yes, resentment—I'm not proud of it, but that's how I felt). I wanted the warts and all account, because I wanted some insight into what might be ahead of us. Why? Not because I'm naturally masochistic, and certainly not because I wanted to dwell on the horror of it, but because I believe that honest insight is essential if we are to create realistic strategies to cope. With no idea what we were facing, I felt cast adrift, with no map, no plan and no idea, really.

I attempted to keep my regular meditation going (and was sporadically successful) and kept reminding myself that it was important to have some down time, time to read, relax and listen to some music. Unfortunately, the reality was that with the increased work schedule and the emotionally and physically torrid hospital schedule, time for me was frustratingly elusive. It was only a matter of time before something had to give.

It gave in the nuclear medicine ward.

I'd never heard of the nuclear medicine ward until the day that we had our first appointment to attend for scans. Even though I'd been closely involved in my friend Helen's breast cancer treatment, until now I'd really only been introduced to chemotherapy wards and oncologists' consulting rooms.

Philip's scans required him to attend for a full day. He needed a lift home, as it was explained he might not be feeling very energetic by the end of the series of tests. (That turned out to be a massive understatement. He was completely exhausted by the time the tests were completed.) Further, the radioactive dye they needed to inject into his system meant that for some hours after, he would be contaminated and needed to avoid contact with pregnant women. As driving himself was considered not an option and travelling by public transport was unviable, it meant that a lift was essential. Naturally, I was that lift.

We had minimum lead-in time for these tests. The week following the diagnosis suddenly filled up with a variety of tests and the scans at the nuclear medicine ward were undertaken on the Wednesday. Ironically, I was scheduled on the same day to offer a workshop on 'managing unexpected change' for one of my regular clients.

I offered to cancel the workshop. I knew the client would understand and it meant I could be at the hospital with Philip. Philip was adamant that I shouldn't cancel. After several conversations I conceded defeat, and the plan was that I would take him to the hospital early, get the run down on times etc., head off and run the workshop, and then return to pick him up.

I had significant reservations about the wisdom of this approach. Running workshops is my profession and what I love doing, but it still demands a high injection of energy on my part. Standing up in front of a group, talking about managing unexpected change while my partner was undergoing tests to check how advanced his cancer was seemed insane to me. Philip's point of view was that if I cancelled he would feel guilty and anyway, in pure practical terms, he pointed out that I'd just be sitting there all day waiting for him and I may as well be doing something that would take my mind off things. I disputed how running a workshop on unexpected change could take my mind off this massive unexpected change in our lives, but I acquiesced because I ran out of energy to discuss it anymore. Anyway, the tests were going to be very expensive, so we really needed the money I would earn.

We arrived at the hospital early. Philip was clearly agitated, and understandably so. I knew he hadn't slept well and understood that with the events of the past few days he had to be exhausted. His normally robust complexion had taken on a grey pallor and his eyes had lost their shine. I knew these were just the physical symptoms of all the emotional stress he was living with, but he looked done in, and I found it hard to contain my tears when I looked at him.

As we entered the hospital, I fiddled with my phone in a bid to comply with the numerous requests to turn off mobile phones posted around the walls. My phone at that time was one of those flip phones that you answer by opening it up. When not in use, the phone was literally folded in half. I flipped the phone open in preparation to turn it off. Philip and I were chatting—I can't remember what about. It was probably something inane and mindless, about anything but the situation we were in. As the phone flipped open, it simultaneously snapped in two. I suspect I'd have been less surprised if I had snapped in two. When it happened to the phone, something inside me gave way. I found the nearest seat, sank into it and dissolved into tears. Waves of sobs burst forth and within seconds I was heaving and gasping, nose running, tears flowing. It wasn't a pretty sight.

Philip looked uncomfortable. I suspected he was embarrassed about such a public display of distress and he didn't know what to do. I didn't know what I wanted him to do, other than the impossible. I wanted him to instantly get well, I wanted to be away from here and I wanted it all to go away. Instead, I held my phone in two parts and kept sobbing.

'We can get a new phone today,' he said. I was speechless. The statement worked. I instantly stopped crying and looked at him incredulously.

'This is not about the fucking phone,' I snapped, feeling instantly guilty, both about the swearing and the snapping. 'Look at where we are. *That's* why I'm crying. I couldn't care less about the phone.' I sniffed and started rummaging through my bag for a handkerchief. Surely I hadn't come to the nuclear medicine ward without a handkerchief, I pondered to myself. What sort of idiot would do that?

Philip handed me a handkerchief from his pocket and continued to outline how we could get a new phone today. He couldn't face the real reason for my tears. He didn't have it in him. He was done. The last five days had taken all he had. The phone was the biggest issue he could manage that day.

I mopped up my face, put the phone pieces in my bag, politely went through the new phone approach with him and collaborated once more in the 'ignore the elephant' strategy. I kissed him goodbye, in a similar way to how I might have kissed him if he was going out to get coffee. I retrieved the car from the car park and headed to town.

I had enough time to drop into the phone shop on the way to the workshop. When asked by a young man if he could help me, I produced the two halves of my phone and said lightly, 'this doesn't seem to work anymore.' He took the phone, understood when I said I was in a hurry, and promised to have a new one ready for me to pick up on my way back. When I picked up the new phone it was fully charged, all my data had been transferred and the phone was fully operational. It was a seamless exchange. That young man, completely anonymous (I can't even remember what he looked like or which store I was in) provided a glorious oasis of ordinary in a barren desert of horror for me that day.

Be prepared to be surprised by
the reactions of others

As the workshop was being offered for an organisation at which I had been employed for many years, it turned out I knew many of the people who attended. It was quite an 'old home week' really, and it was good to see so many familiar faces. It was also hard to put on the front that everything was alright. However, I had made a decision that I wouldn't say anything to the group. This was less about me thinking it was unprofessional and more about my fear that if I opened up I wouldn't be able to contain my emotions and would be unable to run the workshop.

I arrived at the training room. It was a room in which I had attended countless meetings as an employee and I was immediately greeted by a familiar face. 'Pam said to tell you she is just on the other side of that door, and you'd better not leave without saying hello,' he announced, after greeting me warmly. I decided that I had a few minutes to spare before I needed to get organised, so I popped through the door he'd indicated. Sure enough, there was Pam.

I hadn't seen Pam for some time, yet despite that, we slipped easily into conversation. 'How's things?' she enquired.

'Philip's having scans as we speak,' I blurted out. 'Prostate cancer, diagnosis was confirmed last week; we're establishing the extent of the cancer now.'

Pam grabbed a seat and motioned me into it with her eyes. She looked deeply into my face. 'How are you?' she asked.

I could feel my insides churning. I felt sick and bone-shatteringly tired. 'A bit crappy,' I responded.

'Come see me before you leave,' she suggested, then gave me a quick hug and sent me on my way.

I believe the workshop went well. This is my profession and I know I'm good at what I do. I can get into the zone and leave everything else behind and I was able to do that on this day. I remember paying more attention to myself than usual, though. I heard my own words, snippets of advice, quotes, references, and it all seemed helpful. I guess that morning my own work got subjected to the 'cancer' test, and it passed. Even as I write now, I'm proud of what I do and how helpful I know it is, and that morning's workshop was helpful for me.

After we finished, I returned through the door and there was Pam again. The chair that she had previously pulled over for me was tucked in beside her desk and she again motioned me into it. 'I've been doing some research,' she said, and proceeded to offer me information that I hadn't yet heard about, treatment options and management approaches—really, really useful stuff. She advised that her brother-in-law was also living with the same cancer. She understood the seriousness of the situation. She truly acknowledged that what was happening was difficult. I knew then that my decision to go ahead with the workshop was worthwhile because the interaction I had with Pam was helpful beyond belief.

Let me explain why. There are so many myths about cancer and particularly about prostate cancer. The old 'you die with it not of it,' is true in a number of cases, but when a man under 50 is diagnosed with a metastasised Grade 5 cancer, the chances of 'dying with it' are slim and the reality is that the patient is much more likely to die of it. So many people, on hearing that Philip had prostate cancer responded with 'oh, at least it's not serious.' This is a gross misunderstanding. Every year, more men are diagnosed with prostate cancer than women with breast cancer, and the mortality statistics are horrifying. It isn't a 'gentle' cancer. Early in Philip's diagnosis, somebody mentioned to me that prostate cancer is one of the worst to manage. Having now witnessed Philip's experience I would concur with that statement. Ultimately though, it is essential that we all start to take this cancer seriously. It is no more an 'old man's cancer' than Type 2 diabetes is of 'mature age onset'. As with most cancers, the younger you are when you develop it, the more aggressive it is likely to be. Prostate cancer in a younger man is a difficult situation.

I have also found that in our culture (I consider myself British/ Australian) particularly, we don't do emotions well. Dealing with non-physical difficulty is not always our forte. Add to this what I believe is the sometimes misinterpreted positive thinking movement, which is a great ideology but is frequently confused with denial, and we have a cultural propensity to ostrich stance like no other. I wish I had a dollar for everybody who told me to 'think positive'. This is a commendable piece of advice, but has the potential, if not used sensitively, to completely dismiss the feelings of the person experiencing the difficulty and can feel like you're telling them to 'get over it and stop upsetting us.' Yes, I sound harsh. I'm meaning to. As a society we have to get better at being with pain—both our own and other people's. I'm sorry if I sound like I'm on a soap box. It's because I am.

It is rare that I feel murderous; however, if you want to see me and violence in the same room, dismiss me, stomp on my feelings, hold my pain away, and say things like 'think positive' when the world is tumbling down. I'm not talking about missing a sale at Myers (there probably wasn't anything I needed anyway) and I'm not talking about a storm brewing when the washing is out (the clothes will dry later). I'm talking about a diagnosis that has the potential to make me a widow before my first wedding anniversary and people having the gall to look me in the eye and say 'just think positive and it'll all work out.' How I didn't thump them still leaves me amazed.

I truly don't believe anybody deliberately says or does anything to upset us. I really don't. However, in that moment, when we don't know what to do, if we don't stop and think about the consequences, we can say and do really, really stupid things. Before you respond to anybody in pain, STOP!!! Just STOP. Think about what you're about to say and do, and if in any doubt about whether it will be helpful, say and do nothing.

On that day of that first scan in the nuclear medicine ward, the day my phone broke, the day my world felt fragile and unmanageable, Pam was there. She was strong, she was solid, she was caring, she held me, she stood firm in the wake of my tears and she gave me the strength to go back to the hospital, to pick Philip up and to go home knowing that tomorrow was a new day. Thank you, Pam. Sometimes all we ever need is a hug and a gentle ear. We all have the capacity to offer that— we just need to remind ourselves to do it.

Recognise that time is relative

We were back in the urologist's office and he was on thin ice. I watched in disbelief as he threw the envelope holding the test results angrily onto his desk and announced that it was all too late, the cancer had spread. He seemed upset with the cancer for proving him wrong. It was like watching a child throw a tantrum because he is disappointed with his Christmas present. The urologist felt hard done by. First, the biopsies let him down by returning a confirmation of cancer and now the subsequent tests had added further evidence of the depths of his bad call.

So much for all those antibiotics, I thought. While the prescribed drugs were doing nothing but sapping Philip's energy and inviting a numbing level of lethargy, the cancer had been creeping ahead, seeking out bone cells and looking for ways to escape from its initial prison in Philip's prostate. Now it seemed he was carrying a travel bug that could rival the most enthusiastic backpacker on their first Contiki tour. Philip sat next to me oozing vibes of defeat. A cancer metastasised to the bones was a bad situation. We both knew that.

I could hear the urologist rabbiting on. 'I'd suggest surgery immediately. We'll do a radical prostatectomy. You will definitely be left impotent and most likely incontinent; however, you can get pads to put in your underwear to manage that.'

Joan Wilson-Jones

When Philip spoke, it was in a drone-like voice that I'd never heard before. There was no emotion. It was a bland monotone, like the audio equivalent of a flat, barren landscape 'But if the cancer has left the prostate, what's the point of surgery?' he enquired. 'Are there any silver bullets on the horizon?'

The urologist picked up the envelope for the third time and threw it more determinedly back down onto the desk. 'Nothing that will help you.' He finished the sentence with a grunt. 'You could have as little as six months depending on the speed of this— highly unlikely you'll last longer than five years.' With that, he plonked himself down in his chair and looked determinedly at his hands; anything but meet our gaze.

Without further comment, we simultaneously stood up, linked hands and walked out. As we passed the receptionist's desk, Philip stopped, and in the same contourless voice said, 'Please let the doctor know that I don't expect a bill for today.' We left. We didn't need any consultation, the urologist was officially sacked and I was aware that I had just become part of the medical hiring and firing team.

We didn't speak again until long after we got home. On a personality profile, Philip came up as a high introvert and internal processing was his forte. I'm quite the opposite, but I understood and I respected his need for silence. I made a pot of tea, quietly set up a snack on the deck and left Philip with his thoughts. I knew him well enough to know that we would talk when he was able to, when he had had the time he needed to digest and analyse the information we'd just been given. Given the intensity of the information, the only thing I didn't know was how long the silence might be with us for.

I sat in the house and sipped my tea mindlessly. The myriad of conversations held over the preceding few months sparred and vied for air space in my head. The rushes of our personal horror movie jumbled around in my mind. Players kept appearing and statements kept resounding, bouncing off my skull. There was George's voice asking over breakfast, 'How are you, Philip?', the high priestess officiating at our commitment ceremony, 'And now I cast the magic circle'; the nurse at the hospital, 'You take a seat here, Joan, and we'll let you know when he's ready'; and Pam before the workshop, 'And how are you?' Thousands of snippets sped through my brain, all punctuated with, 'You could have as little as six months.' Time had slowed to almost a stop, yet my mind was racing, my surrounds had blurred, life was out of focus and totally unorchestrated. I was in some sort of emotional free fall. The screeching of an ambulance siren brought me back to reality. It sounded close, very close and when I looked out towards the deck, Philip was missing.

I hadn't heard the motorbikes. Maybe they had blended into the mish-mash of conversation racing out of control through my brain. We lived on a country road dotted with lots of curves and corners. The motorcyclists loved it. Philip had once counted 125 Harley Davidsons as they went past. That day there were just two motorbikes and I have no idea what variety they were.

Philip had watched them come around the corner. Later he told me that he had thought to himself as they accelerated out of the corner that he hoped they knew there was another sharp bend just beyond our gate. It seems at least one of them didn't, because he missed the corner and his joy ride and his life were suddenly halted by a tree. Philip didn't hear the crash. The young man died quietly, but Philip heard the ambulance siren some twenty minutes later. True to his style, he donned his volunteer fireman's jacket and went out to help with traffic control while the paramedics did their job. The ambulance left in silence, and Philip returned to his now untouched cold cup of tea. I went to sit with him. He spoke to nobody in particular.

'I watched them come over the hill. They were travelling too fast. Somehow, though, I could sense they were enjoying it. I tried to wave them down, but they didn't see me.' He sighed and started crumbling a biscuit on the plate in front of him. 'I've just been told I might only have six months. That guy had about six seconds when I saw him come flying over the hill. I hope to fuck it was the best six seconds of his life.'

I put my hand on his arm. We were crying in unison, and the tears dropped off our respective cheeks in perfect synchronicity. He looked over at me. 'Whatever time we've got, it is our responsibility to live it.' Some of his old strength had returned to his voice. It was colourful again; alive with tonal hills and valleys. Then the silence returned, but it had changed, just as we had changed.

No longer was it about self-contemplation—now it was for respect. The silence was to honour a young life that had just ended. I wouldn't say we suddenly became more resolved— I'm not sure what we became—maybe resigned, though not defeated. We both knew that we were going to do all we could, but the event we had just witnessed had irrevocably changed something in us.

At our gate after that accident was a constant reminder of the value and precariousness of life. There was a plain white cross, a much-loved dog-eared brown teddy bear and a note from the boy's father that read, 'I told you it was a shit of a bike.' We were both propelled into a journey of living, for whatever time we both had.

Know (regardless of other people's
opinions) that there is no 'right way'

We were weighing up our options and doing our research. Philip was, as always, the quintessential researcher. His thirst for knowledge and information was insatiable and he turned to the computer. I did what I've always done in a crisis. I went looking for books.

We received some interesting reactions from people around us. Some just wholeheartedly supported whatever we did, while others looked on in amazement, clearly convinced that it wasn't the cancer that would get Philip, but insanity. There was disbelief that with a prognosis such as he had, he was wasting time 'doing nothing'. That assumption couldn't have been further from the truth.

People openly questioned our decision not to have the surgery. Even now, I stand firm on the sensibility of that decision. The cancer had spread. Removing the prostate wasn't going to stop the progression of the disease. I was asked about it recently, and my response remains the same. If the cancer had been contained in the prostate, Philip would have been in that operating theatre in a flash. Even with the post-surgical impacts of impotence and incontinence, the surgery would have been worth it if it was going to save his life.

In Philip's situation, surgery didn't have the capacity to be life-saving, just life destroying. His body would have had to recover from major surgical trauma and we wanted to direct that energy towards slowing the cancer down. I suspect many of our friends still believe we rejected medicine and went on our own 'hippie way'. Yes, we were certainly prepared to explore complementary or alternate options, as were we happy to go down a medical path if we could find one that could offer us help. As it turns out, our journey pretty much blended the two approaches.

It was a time of contrasts. On the positive side, my workload was increasing all the time, as my business thrived and flourished. Philip's business, however, languished. He was having trouble securing contracts and had very little work coming in. He was frustrated by this, as he felt the distraction of work would be helpful.

Emotionally, he swung from despondence, to despair, to determination. The mood swings were rapid and I had trouble tracking the changes. His long-term anger bubbled beneath the surface. He had historically been angry about life and now he was angry that he had cancer. To the outside world, though, he was determined to appear in control and, particularly in those early days, I'm sure that most of the people around us saw only the calm exterior that he was so determined to project. The effort to behave as if we were coping often proved too much, and many of our evenings were spent submerged in that deep level of anguish and fear that only impending death can generate.

Philip continued to see our new GP and we looked at diets and lifestyles and researched the full range of options. It was an informative yet exhausting time. It was great to be busy with work, as I knew the financial resources were going to get very stretched, but I was weary from back to back workshops, frequent flights interstate and hours at the computer preparing material. There was no doubt that we were under enormous pressure.

... but be prepared to learn from those
who've been there before you

As the new year kicked over, we were still exploring options. We continued to socialise as much as time and energy would allow, but deep inside we both battled confusion as we attempted to manage the cocktail of emotions that impacted on our days.

We tried to keep busy making plans for the farm. We decided to go ahead with our dream to have animals. 'Life must go on,' we mused on the good days and 'it's important for Philip to see it unfold,' directed us on the difficult days.

I have for some years presented workshops at the Relaxation Centre in Brisbane. A fellow presenter is veterinarian Dr Ian Gawler. Ian's story is remarkable. Given just a few weeks to live at the age of 25, he is now alive and well and in his 60s. He runs cancer management retreats in the Yarra Valley in Victoria.

To date, Ian and my paths had (frustratingly) not crossed, and I was keen to meet the man behind the legend of healing. It definitely wasn't the way I'd planned to meet Ian, but I spoke to Philip about his work and it seemed like a positive next step to go to Gawler.

We participated in the ten day retreat (well nine and a half days really, as the program finished at lunchtime on the final day) and I would highly recommend it to anybody in our situation. I was lucky that they were able to fit me in as well. (Preference is given to people with cancer, though support people are welcome if there is room.)

For me, Gawler offered some hope. For Philip (I found out later), Gawler was something he felt I wanted to do and so he went along. Certainly the ten days could be quite challenging for people not accustomed to Ian's lifestyle or philosophies and I suspect that Philip, on that basis, found it quite difficult.

I'd been a vegetarian for some years, had, as alluded to earlier, a semi-regular meditation practice, and was a committed believer in the concepts of natural healing and the benefits of productively dealing with emotions.

Philip loved a good steak, thrived on red wine and (as also mentioned earlier) was fundamentally angry at life. I'm not sure he was all that comfortable with the Gawler philosophy, but he developed a great regard for Ian. I think Ian's boyish humour really won Philip over.

When I compared the retreat dates to my diary I was delighted to see that I could make nine of the nine and a half days. (Having a nine day clear space at that time was unheard of, so it seemed to me that fate was giving me permission to go.) That I would need to leave very early on the final day to make it to a workshop in Brisbane didn't concern me too much. It was better to do most of it than none of it, was my thought.

I think many of our friends were relieved to see us heading off to Melbourne. As least, in their perception anyway, we were finally doing something. I'm intrigued by the number of people who had assumed that because there were no surgeon's knifes or chemo wards that we were ignoring this cancer. The fact was, surgery wasn't a viable approach and, at that time, we were advised there were no chemotherapy options for Philip's type of cancer.

My dear and close friend Sharon met us at Tullamarine. Sharon had driven down from Wodonga (about four hours north, on the Victorian/New South Wales border), just to pick us up and drive us to the retreat centre in the Yarra Valley (about two hours drive south of the airport). She then repeated the six hour return drive home once she had dropped us off and was returning on the final morning to take me back to the airport, driving back to the centre to collect Philip at lunch time, then taking him to the airport and then driving home. You often hear people say that when a difficult diagnosis comes in they don't know what they can do. I had many friends who really knew what to do, and if driving sixteen hours in one day was something useful, then amazing people like Sharon just did it.

We stopped in the village of Yarra Glen for lunch and Philip set about ordering every meat dish on the menu. He was stocking his body up. If they'd been prepared to serve him a vat of wine to go with his meal, he would have consumed that as well. He was jovial and interactive. He liked Sharon a lot. They shared a deep passion for football and cricket and they could spar off each other for hours. A stranger at a nearby table would have seen three friends laughing and joking. Our capacity as human beings to 'put on a face' is quite remarkable. So much can be hidden by a steak sandwich and a smile.

I love my coffee! Every so often I give up drinking caffeine for a time to ensure that I'm not physically addicted, but despite that, I know without doubt that I have an emotional attachment to a good soy latte. I love the taste, I love the ritual and I love the energy I feel surrounding me when I'm consumed in my coffee bliss. I'm choosey about my coffee (some might say quite snobbish). I have standards and I don't compromise. I need to be sitting down, with time to devote to the enjoyment (no paper cups while running down the street), it needs to be prepared lovingly, and ideally it is shared with good friends (though peaceful strangers also work. Coffee in a coffee shop is always superior when there are others sharing the space.)

I knew there would be coffee at the Gawler Centre and I also knew that I would not be offered any for drinking purposes. Coffee 'Gawler style' isn't taken orally. Demonstrated to be an effective liver cleanser, there was always coffee being brewed, but it was for enemas only. With that in mind, I indulged in two cups of my drug of choice, knowing that it would be ten days before I could return to my much-loved ritual.

The Gawler Centre is basic and comfortable. It's no five star hotel, but it's welcoming and nurturing. I loved it from the start. After the check-in details were completed, we were shown to a sparsely furnished room with boarding school-style twin beds. As Philip's cancer was relatively manageable, we'd been allocated a room without an en-suite and advised there was a communal bathroom facility just down the covered breezeway. (There are limited en-suite rooms and these are naturally given to those whose cancer is more advanced and for whom private bathroom facilities are more necessary.) We had a small patio overlooking the lush green property. The January weather was warm but manageable. All in all, it was pretty idyllic, really. I decided the absence of coffee for oral consumption was a small price to pay for nine days of meditation, fresh food and uplifting lectures and discussions. Having deposited my backpack in the corner, I stepped onto the patio, filled my lungs with fresh air and connected with just how tired I was. This will be great for both of us, I thought. I truly believe it was.

Philip was restless. Only when I discovered later that he'd come along because he thought it would be helpful for me, did I realise that his restlessness was from his lack of ease about being there. Philip had spent a brief time in a monastery between leaving school and turning 20. On reflection, I suspect there was some significant déjà vu happening. The thought of nearly two weeks of meditation, contemplative discussion, abstinence and frill-free vegetarian food was probably pushing some painful historical buttons for him.

Sitting still was never his forte. We travelled extensively throughout our relationship and Philip was forever disappearing on boats and trains. He didn't do 'one place' well at all and our arrival at the Gawler Centre was no different.

While I was taking in the view and calming my energy with some relaxed breathing, he announced that he was going exploring. I decided that what I was doing was best for me, and that if he needed to explore then explore he must. I bade him farewell with a wave of my hand and a knowing smile.

He returned some two hours later, a veritable mine of information. He'd sussed out how many people were participating in the retreat, he had located the creek, he had somehow acquired a map of the local wineries (not that we ever visited them) and he'd met Ian and Ian's wife.

'I met Ruth,' he said.

'Who?' I enquired.

'Ian's wife, Ruth.'

'Ian's wife is Grace.'

'Well somebody had better tell him that. Because he introduced her to me as Ruth.'

Over the years I'd read many of Ian's books, and in the lead up to attending the retreat I'd acquired and listened to the majority of his tapes (all are highly recommended). Through these, I'd developed a sense of Ian and a connection to Grace. Ian's books all acknowledged Grace, who he put on a pedestal of patience and persistence. Grace, through Ian, shone for me as an angel of compassion and emotional equilibrium. She walked beside him through his illness, she never faltered in her strength and resolve and she remained calm and serene throughout the whole, horrendous journey.

Well, that's my interpretation of Ian's account anyway. He summed up his devotion to Grace in the dedication in one of his books—'for Grace, naturally'. Grace had lived up to her name. One of my motivations for coming to Gawler was to meet her. I wanted to talk to her. Did she ever wake up in the middle of the night so angry at the situation that she wanted to scream? Did she ever look at Ian and feel the bitter taste of resentment that his illness was sapping her of her energy and enthusiasm? In short, was Grace really a saint and I a failure, or were lapses into the blazing fires of emotional hell normal? I had to know, and now here I was, all ready to ask, and who the hell was Ruth?

Ruth is Ian's second wife. Grace has gone. Ian survived cancer, but his marriage didn't. On my return to Brisbane I once again started researching. The Gawler marriage wasn't the only one to crash and sink on the rocks of disease. Even just the stats for high profile marriage breakups post-illness are alarming. Add in the hidden figures (the anonymous divorces that we never hear about) and the picture is horrendous—way in excess of the general divorce rates. 'Surviving cancer' suddenly took on a whole new meaning. Any life-changing illness takes more than just the patient. It breaks down relationships (family/romantic/social) because dealing with it 24/7 is so debilitating. Emotions run rampant, connections are severed, patience is eroded and optimism is challenged—for EVERYBODY.

Grace has since written her own account (*Grace, Grit and Gratitude*). It is a raw and painful account of the invisibility that she felt throughout Ian's illness. It is the tears turned to words that the author Paulo Coelho refers to in *Aleph*.

The role of the carer/supporter is complex and lonely. Here is a quote from Grace Gawler that sums it up better than I ever could:

> *I found it demanding to live with a high degree of uncertainty and silence. There was no-one that I could talk to—no shoulder to cry on—no person for me to lean on. I soon discovered that the caring partner's role was precarious and despite the fact that I was an integral part of everything, I remained separated from everything* (Grace Gawler — *Grace, Grit and Gratitude*)

I read it recently and it resonated deeply. As I read, my soul screamed out 'yes!' and I felt somehow connected to that vast community of carers who had all felt so invisible that eventually they had disappeared—into loneliness, into solitude, into divorce or into widowhood.

Listen well, and mind the green juice

Our first meeting with the full group was scheduled for the afternoon of our arrival. We sat around in the obligatory circle, Ian and Ruth forming an equal component yet, for all of us, standing out. A circle doesn't have a front or a back. It doesn't have a start or an end. By its very definition there is no 'special' spot, but as our hosts and facilitators for the next ten days, Ian and Ruth were 'in' the circle but not 'of' the circle.

Philip and I were seated on the left hand side of Ian, and he started the group introductions from his right. As each person spoke, they added their pain and fear to the energy in the room. We were all scared. We had been thrown together by a common demon and yet, of course, we all had our own story.

There was a young, single woman, diagnosed with an aggressive bone cancer on her 27th birthday. We heard a young mother's tearful and frightened account of her fear that breast cancer was going to leave her precious small children motherless. We met a middle-aged man, shrunken behind his anger and disbelief that testicular cancer could be happening to him. Some defaulted to humour, while others just dissolved into tears. There were husbands, wives and partners searching for reassurance and promises. Everybody was in search of hope. We'd all read the miracle stories and we were all present on that day, hoping that ours would be another one to be admitted to that special journal of recovery.

Many of the participants were in pain. Rather than chairs, they occupied cushions on the floor—deep, comfy nests designed to reduce their discomfort. Some had come willingly, others under protest. A beer drinking, steak eating truck driver, diagnosed with advanced pancreatic cancer just hours previously had been brought along by his wife in the hope that they could sidestep the six month sentence that the doctors had delivered to them just the day before.

Every story chipped away at my heart. I saw my daughters in the young women and my mother genes rallied and hijacked my composure. After what seemed like an eternity, it was our turn. I was first.

'I'm here with Philip,' I motioned to my right. Suddenly that felt like all I had to say. After all, our reason for being there was Philip's story and somehow it seemed arrogant for me to try to tell it. I couldn't think of a story for me. I had a role, but not a story, and right at that moment even my role felt undefined. I hadn't yet taken the title of 'carer', and 'support person' sounded too clinical. Words, normally a commodity that flow through me in endless supply, suddenly were glaringly absent. 'We're from Brisbane,' I muttered and with that I glanced over at Philip, hoping he would realise that the baton was now his.

He did. 'I'm Philip,' he announced loudly. He voice sounded strong and robust. 'Prostate cancer I'm told, in the bones now, heading heaven knows where, always thought it was for old guys, been a bit of a shock, to be honest.' With that, he looked at Ian. 'I've decided to try the red wine and sex cure. I think it could be a winner. Ian, what do you think?'

I shrank back into the chair as my insides cringed and churned. Philip's announcement had been full of humour, however the 'joke' was lost on me in the flood of my embarrassment. I looked timidly at Ian, awaiting his response of disapproval.

Instead, Ian's smile was instant and spontaneous. He seemed genuinely amused and I realised that in the meeting a few hours earlier, he and Philip had already made quite a man to man connection. With a slight laugh, he responded 'That's the advanced course, Philip. First, you have to pass carrot juice and meditation.' There was a hum of laughter around the circle and the energy within the group seemed to relax slightly.

The seriousness soon returned as Ian embarked on his welcome speech. He was clear about his objectives for the program. Here is a summary of the things I most related to:

* Ian instructed us to heed the diagnosis and disregard the prognosis. A diagnosis he reminded us had scientific, medical foundations, but the prognosis, he stressed, was a different matter. The prognosis is a 'best guess' from a medical perspective. People defy the prognosis all the time. He suggested that those of us who had been given timeframes sought to disregard them.

* He stressed that the program carried no guarantees. He was direct about the possibility of imminent death for many of us in the room (whether we had received a diagnosis of cancer or not). This program wasn't about how to live longer, he stated, it was about how to live better. For some that might add weeks, months, or even years to their life; for others it might not. Our aim, he reiterated to all of us, was to live well, not just long.

    *   He emphasised the role of allopathic medicine. Don't refuse anything that might help, he implored us. He reminded us that Ruth, his wife, was a GP and was there to help with medications and the administration of chemical pain management. The retreat was 'as well as' any medical pathways we were taking. It was not 'instead of'. 'Medical and non-medical approaches can work hand in hand' said Ian, 'and here at the Gawler Centre we see benefits in both.'

    *   Overwhelmingly though, he advised us to make our own choices. The Gawler approach can feel very challenging to those whose lifestyle isn't already in alignment—no meat, no alcohol, no processed food, no sugars, no added fat. Meals were wholesome and as close to the ground as possible (with ingredients selected and prepared as close to harvesting as could be obtained). As I said earlier, I had been vegetarian for some years, and the shift to being vegan didn't feel overwhelming. But I knew I'd miss some of the much-enjoyed treats like a wine with dinner, chocolate, and my biggest gastronomic weakness of all—chips (a delicious legacy of my England heritage). Despite that, I was excited about the idea of the 10 day cleanse.

Philip, on the other hand, was emitting vibes of tension. He had staunchly refused to join me in my vegetarianism at home, though was mindful not to offer meat to me. For him, the thought of no meat, and to his mind, being force fed tofu for the duration of our stay was, I could tell, unnerving. On conclusion of the outlining of what we could expect to enjoy at meal times, Ian looked over at Philip. 'Mostly though, Philip, I believe that one of the biggest setbacks we can give ourselves in life is to deny ourselves something and then resent it. If you want that steak, have it. Bless it and enjoy it, for eaten with joy and happiness, the steak is much better for you than the tofu eaten with resentment and anger. However, I need to repeat, there won't be any steak here.' He smiled again and then went on to outline the program for the rest of the retreat, encourage us all to enjoy the tranquillity of the grounds and gardens, and remind us that the first formal session would be held after dinner that evening.

The time at Gawler was fascinating and distressing. To bear witness to such emotional, physical and psychological pain was almost unbearable, yet the atmosphere and ambience were incredibly soul-restoring and nurturing. It was an emotional anomaly of gargantuan proportions. Each day started with an early meditation session followed by a wholesome breakfast. Meal times were punctuated with 'lectures' (offered by Ian and an array of guest speakers). There was generous time for relaxation, regular meditation throughout the day and what felt like an endless stream of juices.

The worst of the juices was a green concoction offered a few times a day. I enjoyed all the other juices, but the 'green' juice was rather unpalatable in my view. I was here for the whole experience though, and I persevered for well over a week before I conceded defeat and opted to leave the green juice alone.

Philip speculated loudly and endlessly on the origins of the green juice (my understanding is that it was a combination of a variety of leafy green vegetables), pondering with each serving whether we had inadvertently landed ourselves in the 1973 science fiction movie *Soylent Green*. His continual insistence that, like the movie, this green juice was actually prepared by putting old people in the blender, did nothing to convince my taste buds that they could welcome the beverage. As I write, my mind also wanders spontaneously to accounts I read during this time of cancer patients putting raw liver in the blender and drinking the resulting concoction. I'm aware of a slight wave of nausea. At desperate times, all of us might try desperate things.

I won't recount the entire time at the Gawler Centre, but a couple of things remain highlighted for me, so I'll share them.

One night, the guest speaker was a man by the name of Dr Avni Sali. He was the Director of the Graduate School of Integrative Medicine, Melbourne. (There are a number of references to him and his work on the net; I would encourage you to browse through them.) He was a highly informative and entertaining speaker, and I found his approach to the validity and wisdom of integrating allopathic and complementary approaches inspiring. He was a passionate and compassionate medico who used caution with prescriptions and advocated the body's capacity to heal itself when presented with an environment conducive to such an event.

Of all the speakers I heard and sessions that I attended during my time at the Gawler Centre, Avni's was by far the most memorable for me. Ian's approach could be described as bordering on fanatical (and justifiably so) but I responded positively to the more relaxed perspectives offered by Avni.

Trained in traditional medicine, he opened his presentation by confessing to having a dream to train doctors to not need a prescription pad at all—with two exceptions. 'When I first meet a patient with cancer,' he explained, 'I write them two prescriptions: 1. Get a dog! Research shows that people with dogs live longer and 2. Go to the movies! It's like taking an overseas trip.'

Contrary to Gawler philosophies, Avni advocated a glass of wine with dinner and, like Ian, he stressed the importance of living a fulfilling, fun-filled life. This speaker resonated strongly with me. The entire time that I spent at the Yarra Valley centre has continued to have an impact on how I approach and live my life. However, it was that the one evening with Dr Avni Sali that changed me immeasurably. There are moments in our lives that stand out. They glow as beacons lighting up our future. That evening was one of those times for me, and I realised as I sat in the audience that my purpose in coming to Gawler had been fulfilled.

The people at the retreat also had an overwhelming impact on me. Sometime before going to the Gawler Centre, I had trained in the energy exchange modality of Reiki, and I willingly and happily offered my hands to any who wanted to experience/re-experience this process.

The young woman with bone cancer approached me almost immediately. She told me that it had been some months since she had slept well. Despite massive doses of pain relief medication, her pain levels throughout the night chased sleep away. She looked drawn and pale, and she was the same age as my younger daughter. I connected fiercely with her and we worked together daily. The Reiki sessions extended into conversations about her life, her dreams and her fears. She touched my soul deeply.

The morning after her first Reiki session I watched with delight as she glided into the breakfast room. She came over and sat beside me. 'You look good,' I noted.

'I slept,' she whispered, almost as if scared to say it too loud in case she broke some magic spell. She hugged me lightly and reached for the porridge.

On returning to Brisbane and talking with a client about the Gawler process, it turned out that the client was a close friend of this young woman's parents. The following year, when I was back in America for our second contract with *Summer Arts*, I was devastated to receive an email from the client advising that this beautiful young woman, with so much to live for, had lost her battle with this aggressive, cruel disease. She didn't see her 30th birthday. I sat that night and wrote to the young woman's parents and received a beautiful reply from them. I still think of her often, when I'm facing adversity, when I'm feeling fed up, and when I forget the resolutions I made while at Gawler. She is a special angel in my story. Our paths crossed briefly, and in reality I knew only snapshots of her, but her memory reminds me how much impact we can all have. With that knowledge comes a responsibility for all of us to give it our all.

I guess those are the moments and memories from Gawler that I packed into my backpack and loaded silently into Sharon's car in the darkness of the pre-dawn on the morning of my departure. My bag felt light and my heart heavy when I touched down in Brisbane and realised I had less than 15 minutes to complete a 30 minute journey across Brisbane to start a workshop of a whole different kind. I felt confused and jumbled. The Gawler experience had smashed through some deep, reinforced vaults and an array of emotional vampires had been dragged from the dark crevices of my unresolved history. The process encourages dealing with past hurts and painful memories through understanding and forgiveness (not by dwelling on or reliving — an important differentiation). While remarkably therapeutic, such a process is not undertaken without difficulty. This high road to healing has, I believe, the capacity to be beneficial for anybody who has the courage to undertake it. As a result of many hours of release work and self-nurturing, many of my demons of the past now lay slain, the stakes of understanding and resolution driven through their hearts, but others lingered, unravelled and unrestrained, taunting me to deal with them. I sank into the seat of the taxi and reminded myself that I had whatever time the drive took to pull myself together.

Count your blessings

The taxi ride from the airport to the conference rooms in Spring Hill was slowed by both the peak hour traffic and the interminable whingeing of the taxi driver. My patience was already pretty thin as a result of that morning's 2.00 am start, coming heavily on the back of the emotional farewells with the group the night before. It could be said that I was tired and emotional, in the literal sense of the term.

The taxi driver droned on about the hot weather, the traffic and the annoying passengers. His list of upsets was endless, and in my somewhat pensive state of mind, all his complaints seemed minor and pointless. Yes, it was hot; it was summer for heaven's sake! Of course the traffic was slow, it was 8.30 am on a Friday morning—and I strongly suspected that his passengers were unfriendly because he had exhausted them.

I lapsed into strategic umming and ahhing. It was all I could manage. I didn't trust myself with words. If I broke into language, I feared I'd regress into an emotive account of my experiences over the past nine days, concluding with a lecture on how he needed to count his blessings and stop moaning. I maintained my silence for the entire journey and on arrival at my destination, couldn't wait to get out of the taxi.

Brisbane looked different. I'd been away less than two weeks, but somehow, in that small window of time, it had changed immeasurably. I couldn't tell you specifically how. Was it greyer, duller? I'm not sure. It seemed bland, somehow—like life was rehearsed and practised, a monotonous movie playing outside the car window; not real, somehow.

I've had extensive periods of time away from Brisbane over the years. These included a whole year backpacking the world. What a lot of adventures that year had held. I also had ten exciting months living in France. Always when I returned from a lengthy absence, it was like I had to rediscover Brisbane—or maybe I had to rediscover myself. I was used to the 'culture shock' of returning (as defined and disturbing as any culture shock of arriving in a new place). But I could never have imagined that a mere nine days away could elicit the same impact as several months. The impact of the retreat was really starting to make itself known to me.

I started to realise that it is quite a journey back from an experience such as the Gawler Centre. For nine days I had been with a group of people trying hard to 'live'. Not just be alive for a bit longer, but doing all they could to live in the moment they were in. They were facing death, that unknown destination that we are all racing towards (yet most of us fail to acknowledge most of the time). At the same time, they were striving wholeheartedly to live life.

Buddhist monks and nuns meditate on death as a way to embrace life. However, my time at a cancer retreat reinforced for me that until there is a signal of certainty, the speculation is still rather academic and we can push the thought to one side. I was with the people facing this certainty, but I wasn't one of them. My encounter was one step removed, and I suspect the impact was diluted as a result. Even watered down, though, the experience was confronting and challenging.

I was reminded of an experience I'd had some years earlier. I was ambling along a Brisbane street in the heart of the city. A major construction was taking place and I passed the building site without taking too much notice of anything. I was in a hurry and was focused on my destination. I passed the construction and was pleased when the traffic lights at the adjoining intersection turned green for pedestrians just as I approached it. I crossed the intersection at a half jog and just as I landed on the opposite side there was a massive noise accompanied by fierce shaking of the ground underneath me.

Part of the building under construction had collapsed, trapping a number of people under the rubble—people who were walking where I had been walking, seconds before. I still remember vividly the screams and shouts, the confusion and panic. The sounds of human terror were quickly drowned out by the sounds of emergency vehicle sirens. It was a fatal accident, and there was a young child among the dead.

A confrontation with sudden death in this way is horrific, unbelievable. People who were there a few seconds ago, blissfully unaware of what their next step would bring them, were suddenly gone. We all have stories of being T-barred (crashed into) in these sorts of ways. The collision scratches us deeply.

When a diagnosis of a potentially fatal cancer is received by somebody close to you, there is the dual difficulty of dealing with the potential loss of that person and the ear-splitting crash as we are once again T-barred by the reality that death awaits us all (because none of us are getting out of this life alive).

The experience at the Gawler Centre had been intense. The program is designed to help you confront and accept your own mortality. If we allowed ourselves to dwell on it too much, we would all have the potential to be challenged by the reality of our unavoidable eventual demise. We are all going to die.

Despite this, we launch into each day expecting to survive to the evening and beyond. (We demonstrate this by making dinner plans, organising the weekend and booking future holidays.)

To not do this would likely drive us to insanity (and create massive disruption, to say nothing of a potential lack of meals). As I sat in that taxi and listened to the driver drone on and on about the weather and the bad attitudes of his passengers, I thought again of that young boy under the rubble. My mind also drifted to the motorcyclist who had died outside our house just weeks earlier and I thought of the people I'd met at Gawler. The intense realisation of the inescapability of my own death washed over me, and I felt somehow irretrievably altered.[1]

Joan Wilson-Jones

Endnote

[1] *Many years ago I attended a fourteen day program on living and dying facilitated by Dr William Bloom. The program was held in the picturesque central highlands of Scotland (at the Findhorn Foundation). In one exercise William had us all visualise our 'perfect death' and naturally we all conjured up images of ourselves in advanced years, faculties intact, slipping gently away surrounded by family and friends: the 'ideal demise'. Completing the exercise felt nurturing and quite peaceful. Later, one of my fellow participants referred to the exercise during our conversation after dinner. 'Complete waste of time if you ask me,' she said, her strong Belfast accent adding a musical lilt to the sentence. 'I go to a funeral at least once a week and most of the poor bastards have been shot down in the street. They die writhing in pain and screaming in anger. It's not a peaceful process, Joan; death is not a peaceful process.' I guess that is why most of us, deep down, are terrified about it and why on hearing a difficult diagnosis, we waver between sadness for the person diagnosed and paralysing terror in case the next one is us.*

Keep dancing—even if you don't like the tune

Philip returned home later that night. His mood was upbeat and he looked stronger and felt more alive and present than he had. Strength had returned to his voice and he seemed to be bubbling over with ideas, commitments and motivation. We talked over dinner about the people we had met at the Gawler Centre and both agreed that the retreat had been a helpful thing to do.

'I've asked the universe for a sign that I'll get better,' Philip announced over a cup of herbal tea. 'And I've asked her to send me a koala,' he concluded.

'I'm not sure you are supposed to dictate to the universe,' I responded, amused that, after years of mocking my proclamations of universal connection, Philip had now suddenly decided to get into 'signs' and taken it upon himself to change the rules.

'Well I was concerned that if I didn't stipulate, she might get it wrong. This way we're both clear—I want a koala.'

'Well, let's see what happens then,' I concluded. We started setting out our new plans for how our life would look post the Gawler experience.

Philip launched into our new regime immediately on waking the next morning. His first task was to dramatically dispose of the microwave oven. I had refused to have a microwave for many years and had been none too happy some months earlier when Philip's had been ceremoniously installed in our new house.[2]

'No,' I had said, glaring at the offending appliance.

'Yes,' he replied emphatically. 'Love me, love my microwave.' He had looked over and smiled at me. 'What's the problem with them?'

'Where do I start?' I murmured. With every point of concern I raised, he countered with 'where's the proof?' I made for the computer, determined to bring up research and references, but everything I found he had discounted. He remained focused intently on the plugging-in process.

'Ok,' I said, 'I can compromise. Please don't put my food in it, and can I ask you not to use it while I am in the kitchen?'

'Deal!' he stated excitedly and promptly asked me to step outside while he zapped some frozen bread to make a sandwich.

The microwave had remained until that morning and I watched as he, with the same diligence that he had displayed when he installed it, removed it from its 'cubby' and carried it to the garage.

I decided that, in this instance, discretion was the better part of valour and despite being as inclined to 'I told you so' as anybody, was happy to quietly relish this moment without words. The kitchen was again microwave-free. That felt good.

Philip advised that Ian had been as emphatic as I about the dangers of microwave ovens, but his references and research were more convincing than mine. I didn't care how it happened;

I loved the idea that the 'nuke machine' had gone and, as an extra bonus, I had space for some cookbooks in the kitchen. (Microwave portals make great bookcases).

Of course, we didn't just fall back into life. We were different. Cancer had changed us both, and so had the Gawler Centre. My previous vegetarianism morphed into veganism and we started juicing with gay abandon. (Not the green juice, though. I couldn't face it and Philip was still attached to his *Soylent Green* theory.) Friends produced a *Champion* juicer (a brand highly recommended by Gawler) they had bought some time ago on eBay and never used. They sold it to us at the bargain price they had procured it for and so we were off and running in the 'dance with cancer'.

Philip and I both agreed that we didn't want to fight this disease. Fighting, for us, felt too violent. It didn't sit right with our pacifist ideals. Also, in all of my reading of stories of survival I had found many disparities in the approaches survivors had taken, and I found only one similarity.

People survived cancer by being vegetarian, vegan and meat eaters, some put meditation as the primary reason for their cure and others committed to therapy to exorcise their anger and past hurts. The stories, when compared, offered a mish-mash of approaches with one common thread in my view. The survivors had all accepted their illness. They had accepted the possibility of their early demise, they had put things in order, they had made the adjustments to their lives that felt authentic and wholesome for them and then they had just got on and 'danced'.

They went about their lives; they 'sang their own song'. Many found sassiness in themselves that they had never been aware of before; others became committed to a cause and poured themselves into it fully. They lived their own truth and they enjoyed life, not because they might not have much of it left, but because they just decided they loved life. They danced *in spite of* cancer, not *because* of it.

I think that's the ideal, that dance of acceptance, and there are many stories of 'spontaneous remission' that are highly motivating. I guess the dilemma is, how do you do it? Philip paid lip service to the 'dance'; he tried desperately to learn the steps, and I take my hat off to him for his efforts. But when his guard was down, his anger burst forth. Philip was angry before he got cancer and now he was even angrier. Also, which I suspect was of even more importance, he wasn't able to accept or articulate his anger because he was too busy pretending he was coping.

Many around us saw the smiling face. 'Isn't Philip doing well?' they commented. 'He'll be fine with that attitude.' They didn't see the evening rages, the tears, the heavy drinking and the deep, deep sadness. They didn't know of his disappointments in his own life, or of his feelings of being a victim since his childhood and his deep sense of being unloved and unlovable. In fact, he was very lovable. He was a very popular man who made a huge difference to a lot of peoples' lives.

I'd love to say that life became easier when we got back from Gawler, but in actual fact the roller coaster was quickly ramped up as the juices and the organic vegan diet became just more things for Philip be angry about. His anger grew and festered, and the dance steps became convoluted and confusing. We were both constantly tripping up and falling over each other. All too often, there was no rhythm and no grace. We both came to realise that it was a very difficult dance indeed.

Endnote

2   *Over the past few years I had attended many courses and read a number of books and articles that had convinced me to stop using a microwave oven. I'm not certain that all of the accounts that I read would survive rigid scientific scrutiny, but intuitively I felt strongly that I no longer wanted to subject my food to this method of cooking or reheating. I then read the work of Dr Masaru Emoto ('The Hidden Messages in Water' and other titles) and this confirmed my decision. Emoto has developed a way of freezing and photographing water crystals that shows a distinct difference between the beautiful patterns of water cooked gently and lovingly, as compared to the fuzzy, malformed crystals of water heated in a microwave. Emoto's work was the final confirmation for me, and I have not owned a microwave oven since. I recommend his books. They provide wonderful ideas and insights into living more lovingly and the photographic evidence of his crystal images is beautifully illustrative.*

Buy a puppy (or two)

The determination and direction that we gained from Gawler was hard to maintain. Philip was never comfortable with the diet and was vocal in his upset at the lack of a good steak. We were both still feeling pretty much adrift with no medical options to run to. This was a situation we both found unnerving. Philip was naturally anxious and he oscillated between anger, withdrawal and gutsy efforts to get on with life. Every day felt pretty challenging for us as we sought to manage fears and pain.

Nothing is all bad though, and despite all this, areas of life were unfolding in pretty interesting ways. There was lots that was gloriously enjoyable and I worked hard to keep the joys separate from the muck and grime of the challenges we were facing. Our new home felt exciting, with lots of projects to undertake and a glorious degree of natural tranquillity and comfort.

The house frequently rang with laughter and we were blessed with lots of wonderful visitors, often bearing lovingly home-cooked meals. On our return from Gawler, friends had clearly researched his food suggestions, as our table was frequently filled with glorious offerings from the Gawler cookbook.

Avni Sali's advice rang constantly in my ears and, given that we'd decided to progress our plans for a small but interesting menagerie, I was keen to get started on the What If Farm project. I was feeling a bit like a disorientated hiker on an uncertain bush walk in a dark forest with no map or compass, and I was stuck for what to do or where to turn. Filling my life and the property with the joy of animals appealed greatly as a potentially healing project.

As a very young child I had 'befriended' (I'm not sure the other party would see it that way) a woman who ran a small dairy farm near where we lived. I idolised Janet and I have consciously and sub-consciously modelled many aspects of my life on what I believe I saw in her way back then. I was nearly five and had started to drop into her farm on a daily basis to 'help'. Can a five year old actually be of any 'help'? I suspect not, but Janet always made me feel welcome and I'd follow her around like a devoted puppy and marvel at her life, which to me was amazing and enviable.

The days would pass quickly as we busied ourselves bringing the cows in and she'd do the milking, we'd check fences and we'd haul hay. I have no recollection of ever seeing anybody else at Janet's farm. It appeared to me that she ran and managed it completely alone and a part of me resolved then that when I grew up I was going to be like Janet. In many ways she sparked the feminist in me, though I suspect that wasn't a term she had ever heard of. I have no idea of Janet's story. Did she choose to run a farm on her own, or was it a legacy of some painful separation via either divorce or death? I don't know. Did she wake up every morning excited about the prospect of another day of toil, or was she broken by the physical effort and driven on purely from need to carve out a living? I have no idea. I do know that Janet provided an amazing role model. She was, in my mind, a pioneer in the land of 'Sisters are doing it for themselves'.

Just before my fifth birthday, Janet's Border Collie bitch had puppies. They were the most adorable things I have ever seen. My five year old heart was stolen forever and the Border Collie is still the only dog I would consider owning. I must have driven my parents mad harping on about these puppies. They consumed me and took over my conversation from the moment they were born. Each morning the thought of them propelled me from my bed and I'd run as fast as my little legs would go to get to Janet's to be with the puppies. I would have to be prised from them each evening and sent home for dinner.

I remember my dad coming home on the evening of my fifth birthday. Birthdays have always been big in my family and I can still see, like it was only yesterday, dad's beaming face as he strode through the door. 'Happy birthday!' he sang out, and my eyes fixated on the pulsating bulge in his jacket. Something was tucked into his shirt. Exactly on cue, a tiny black and white head popped out and collided gently with Dad's chin. A puppy! He had a puppy—a black and white puppy, a Border Collie! Janet said you and this one had quite bonded,' he laughed as the puppy started licking his chin furiously. 'She said you'd even named this one.'

I had. This was Trixie and she was my first Border Collie. I had my very own dog. I was the happiest kid on the planet.

With Avni's motivating session driving us forward, we both knew that the first arrivals at What If Farm had to be puppies. For me, the word 'puppy' and 'Border Collie' are synonymous. It was not a question of 'if', it was purely a conversation about 'when?' and 'where from?'

Philip, a genuine animal lover, relished the thought of having a dog and willingly supported me in my choice of breed, proclaiming that he'd be happy so long as whatever we choose was a medium to large breed with a friendly nature and lots of energy. On hearing his requirements I quickly confirmed that a Border Collie would definitely fit the bill perfectly for both of us.

I had been shopping on this particular Saturday morning and was returning to the farm through the village of Samford. At Cedar Creek my eyes spotted a sign: 'Border Collie puppies for sale'. The car almost involuntarily turned towards the gate nominated by the sign, but I managed to keep it pointing forward and headed home. I had a horse riding lesson that afternoon and was pushing a bit for time.

A few hours later, as I was relaxing over a well-earned cup of tea, Philip arrived home.

'Did you come through the village?' I enquired nonchalantly.

'Nope, came over the mountain, why?' he replied, somewhat intent on examining his finger tips

'Border Collie puppies for sale at Cedar Creek'

'That's nice. Pity we don't have fences.'

'I know, but we could look.'

'Look?' His focus left his fingertips and he cast a glance into my cup. 'More tea?'

'Ummm, ok, yes. Just look.'

'Ok then,' he put down the kettle he was about to fill. 'I'll get the cheque book.'

'I said just look!' I insisted, rushing to put my cup in the sink and preparing to leave before either of us changed our mind.

'That won't happen,' he grinned, 'but before we get there, we agree on how many and stick to that.'

The litter was eight puppies in all. There were three classic black and white and five with mottled noses and feet. We met the mother first, an almost pure black Border Collie. Dad wasn't there, but we were assured he was of the classic black and white appearance. Both parents were working dogs, and no pedigrees were involved.

On command, eight balls of fluff charged out of the old chicken house that had been their birthing space and was their current home. They circled us, running around us for a few laps. Rosie broke ranks first and headed straight for Philip. I melted as I saw the beaming smile on his face as he bent down to lift her up. She licked his face madly, wriggling with joy in his arms. 'Well, I guess this one wants to come home with us then.' He finished his sentence to the puppy. 'Is that right then? Are you coming home with us?'

We had agreed on two puppies, either a male and a female or two females. I have never had a male dog, so was leaning towards two females, but Harry successfully challenged that as he raced over and seated himself gently but determinedly on my foot. (I have since learnt this is dominant behaviour, but it seemed very cute to me at the time.) I picked him up and fell headlong into his enormous dark eyes. Despite the fact that Harry has turned out to be a chronic licker (a habit I still haven't been able to sway him from—visitors to the farm always get a bath before they are allowed in), he didn't attempt to lick my face that day. He simply sighed (he is a big sigher) snuggled into my arms and looked up at me. In that instant, I knew Harry was also meant to share this journey with us.

Despite the order in which they came to us, Harry became officially Philip's dog. He was to be an incredible source of support to us, and one of Philip's main and most constant companions throughout his illness. Rosie became my dog. We called her 'Nurse Rosie' as during times when Philip was bedridden, she insisted on whoever was home with him doing regular 15 minutes checks. (She resorted to tugging at clothing if said person didn't respond instantly to her silent pleads.) I have always found it fascinating how, despite being purchased together, they immediately worked out the alliances. In the evening when Philip and I would take up our respective after dinner relaxation spots on the couches, Rosie would automatically curl up with me and Harry always positioned himself next to Philip.

As we prepared to leave with our two new family members, the breeder took Philip aside. 'Can I just have a few minutes with her?' he asked, reaching out for Rosie. 'She's my favourite. I just want to say goodbye.' He returned with tears in his eyes. 'Look after them, won't you? If they don't work out, bring them back; we'll always take them back.' He cast a glance my way. Harry was still snuggled tightly in my arms. 'He's a handful,' he noted. 'If you can't cope, we will take him back and you can take another one.'

I never asked what he meant by 'handful' but I would have to say Harry has been by far the easiest dog to raise. Rosie, cute and mischievous as she is, is not only the dominant dog, but generally the one you can rely on to cause a ruckus. Harry, placid by nature, brought an air of calm with him to the farm and that calm remains now. They are gorgeous dogs and beautiful, loyal and incredible friends.

Was Avni's prediction right? That people with dogs live longer has been statistically supported, but has the presence of Harry and Rosie added even a second to our lives? We will never know. But I know for sure, without doubt, that every second with Harry and Rosie has brought endless joy and total unconditional love into our lives and our home.

Connect with others

'Synchronicity' is one of my favourite words. I believe I have experienced alignments in my life that felt way too orchestrated to be simply coincidence. Our next medical exploration was to come from one of these aligned events.

I remember the man in the workshop well. He was stocky in build, not overly tall and carried the expression of someone who was fed up with life. He sat in the middle of the room—not at the front, not at the back. He seemed to be hoping that he would blend into the furniture somehow.

Throughout my presentation, he hung his head heavily. I suspected that he had found it difficult to look life in the face for some time. He didn't respond physically or verbally to anything I said initially, but as the presentation continued, I noticed his body language changing subtly. They were almost indiscernible changes, and I only noticed because I was watching intently. There was something about this man and his responses that suggested to me that, despite his best efforts, he was inadvertently connecting to some of the things I said. I also saw how painful that connection was, and I was overwhelmed by a sense of his need for caring and nurturing.

When he finally spoke, it was to question everything I had said, but his questioning lacked any defiance. It was less about not believing me and more about feeling helpless in the face of the suggestions I was making.

'Sometimes nothing we do changes things,' he murmured, only just audible enough to be heard. 'No matter how much we try, there are things that we just can't alter; things that are going to happen anyway.'

'That's true,' I responded. 'Life doesn't always follow our script and often we are at a loss as to how to manage whatever we are experiencing.' I stopped for a while to observe him. He had raised his head slightly and turned one ear towards me. 'I'm not sure we're meant to control everything; however, what I'm suggesting is that even in the darkest moments, there can be anchors for us to hold fast to. Those anchors are frequently found through our thoughts, our perspectives and our beliefs.'

The man sighed loudly and with the out breath came a waft of deep, deep pain. I knew he had a story, a current story and I could sense that he needed space and time. This man must not be pushed, of that I was certain.

'Life deals up some rough cards,' I continued gently, 'and our job is to somehow play them to the best of our ability. It's not easy and it doesn't always bring what we want, but at the end of the day, the thing we have control over is whether we play the ace or the two, the queen or the joker.'

He repositioned his head so he could closely examine the area of floor between his feet and he sighed again. I watched him as I continued. Questions were coming at me quickly from the group now and I was engaged in responding to them. Despite that, my gaze regularly turned his way.

When the break came, I made a cup of tea and wandered off towards the window on my own. I noticed the man approaching me, and I completed the half turn it took to face him.

'I hear what you are saying,' he said, 'but sometimes it's hard, really hard, to maintain a view that we can do something when it seems there is nothing that can be done'.

I concurred completely with him and my mind wandered to my own life, to the medical desert we were currently occupying. Now it was my turn to sigh.

'My wife has ovarian cancer.' His voice was faint, diluted by the oceans of tears he had already cried. 'It's advanced and the prognosis is poor. Surely you aren't suggesting that if I think positive it will go away?'

'Not for a second.' I moved my cup from my left hand to my right hand, just for something to do. 'It isn't always about making it go away; that is often out of our control and our influence. What I'm suggesting is that even in the mire of this terrible situation, there are things that you can do that can be helpful to you both. There are moments you can savour, memories you can relish, laughter that can still be shared and, who knows, maybe the story will unfold in ways that are much better than any doctor has predicted. However, that's not what this is about. What I'm talking about is living in the present moment and making IT count, so no matter how many moments all of us have, we can make them the best they can be. And yes, sometimes even at their best, the moments are difficult.'

I waited for him to respond, but it appeared that words were beyond him. At this point I decided to break my own rule and share my story. I had to be careful though, as I didn't want it to appear that I was in any way competing. Individual pain needs to be honoured. Life isn't a poker game where we can see your sadness and raise the stakes with a double dollop of grief.

'I have no idea how this must feel for you,' I started, 'though I know how scared I am with every pain, every twinge, and every test.' I explained about Philip's prostate cancer and how we found ourselves in medical no-man's land, too advanced for surgery, no real chemotherapy options at this stage. 'It's terrifying, isn't it?'

I looked into his face and could see he was trying hard not to cry. I looked down. 'Sometimes, I can just remember that however the story is going to unfold, to live this minute, to notice the sunrise, to smell the flowers—I know it sounds clichéd, but in reality, the only power we have is the power to be here now and to take from each moment any gifts it offers, no matter how miniscule those gifts might feel.'

He sighed again. I got the impression that sighing had become his coping mechanism. Then he looked me in the eyes and said, 'Thanks, I think I'm getting what you are saying. I'm sorry for what's happening for you.'

'It's crap, isn't it?' I responded. 'But it's where we are, and all we can do is try to make the best of it that we can.'

At the end of the workshop he came over again to say goodbye. This time his shoulders were back and his eyes were more alive; he managed a half smile and he handed me a piece of paper. 'My wife has found this doctor really helpful,' he said. 'He's a GP with qualifications in diet and nutrition, he specialises in cancer and he seems like a great guy.'

I took the details. 'Thanks,' I said.

'It sounds like you need the next step,' he continued. 'Maybe this guy can help. Good luck.' 'Same to you,' I responded, as he left. And with that he walked out of my life.

When I got home, I told Philip the story and handed him the piece of paper. The doctor was in Brisbane, near the Roma Street Transit Centre. Philip seemed interested and I was pleased the next day when he said he'd phoned and made an appointment. We were back on the medical trail, but this felt like a whole new direction.

It was.

Recognise that not all doctors are wrong

Philip raved about the new doctor when he came home. 'I think he and Ian Gawler are in cahoots!' he exclaimed. 'And he seemed pretty happy when I outlined our approach with food and juices so far.'

I was pleased that a medico had approved of our lifestyle approach.

The new doctor had ordered a raft of general health tests, and Philip had gone straight from his surgery to the pathology lab. He had an appointment the following week to discuss the results.

'Want me to come with you?' I enquired.

'Nope, I'm good to go alone,' was his reply. His voice held a lightness I hadn't heard for some time, 'I like this guy,' continued Philip. 'I think we're on a positive track here'.

The test results were pleasing, and Philip recounted to me later that the doctor had been impressed. Philip was now heading towards his 50th birthday and in the doctor's words, 'These are the test results of a 35 year old man, Philip. The good news is, your body is the worst possible environment for this cancer.' We were both somewhat excited by that news. Our approach so far, it seemed, had been successful in establishing a garden that was primed for good health to flourish. We took great heart from that.

Some fine tuning was made to Philip's (and by default my) diet, and in addition, the new doctor suggested Philip see a specialist radiology oncologist (Dr James). An appointment was made for the next week, and this time I did go with him. We arrived at the Wesley Hospital feeling more hopeful than we had felt for some time. I took it as a positive omen that the waiting time to see Dr James was so short that I didn't have time to assess the quality of the magazines.

Dr James welcomed us both into his consultation rooms. In stark contrast to the sacked urologist, his rooms were orderly and tidy and devoid of other people's files. I instantly warmed to this young, rather gaunt-looking man, despite his propensity to address all his questions to either his computer or the space on the floor between his feet. He seemed uncomfortable with conversation, but very knowledgeable about cancer. I decided the former could be managed easily if he proved to be as competent in the latter as he appeared.

He went through Philip's medical history with patience and diligence and asked lots of questions about our experience at the Gawler Centre. 'I've had many patients get good results from Dr Gawler's approach,' he advised the carpet, 'and I wholeheartedly support what you are doing.'

'Ah,' I mused to myself. 'A doctor on our wavelength. This relationship has promise.'

In addition to advising us to keep doing what we were doing, he concurred with the referring GP's conclusion that, the cancer aside, Philip was a model of exceptional good health. He also suggested that we add the administration of some hormone therapy to the mix.

Prostate cancer is a testosterone-fed cancer. Not too long before Philip's diagnosis, a common treatment was surgical castration in a bid to reduce the testosterone production and seek to effectively starve the cancer. Medical science had advanced recently, and the hormone treatment that Dr James was suggesting was a chemical castration that, unlike its surgical counterpart, could be reversed should a remission be effected.

He presented us with significant research and the possibility of some quite pleasing results. I liked how this doctor didn't push. He informed, he was very detailed with his information (all delivered to the carpet, but easily heard and understood by us) and then he suggested time to think. Nothing was rushed here. Both Philip and I were fully involved in discussions and decisions. In fact, it was evident that this doctor considered Philip to be the conductor. He saw that he (as the doctor) and I had major roles as significant musicians but essentially anything that happened treatment-wise was Philip's call. I liked his humility, I appreciated his understanding and I was amused by his lack of social skills.

Philip and I chatted on the way back to the car and we both felt strongly that this was the right specialist for us. A further appointment the following week saw us signing up for hormone treatment and the conversation we had around the commencement of treatment saw Dr James soar even higher in our esteem.

'What sort of side effects can I expect?' enquired Philip

'I've no idea,' responded Dr James, this time to his computer screen. 'The drug comes with a long list of potential side effects, but in reality we can't predict them, especially with the first administration. It's not good to expect something to go awry; such thinking can create problems.' He handed Philip a business card. 'I'm here business hours,' he explained, 'and my home number is also on this card. If you have concerns, just call me and we can discuss what is happening and determine whether it is the drug or something else. Let's not pre-empt problems; let's see what happens.'

My spirits were flying; I was in medical heaven. We had found our oncological soul mate and we were heading forward. For the first time in many months, a feeling that had become almost alien to me crept back in and took a seat in the back row. Hope had returned, and in the hands of Dr James I felt like we were going somewhere.

Ride the hormone swings and roundabouts

Sue-Ellen and I were invited back to complete another month at CalState University. We were very excited.

Our introduction to *Summer Arts* the year before had provided an amazing month of activity and fun and just prior to just finishing the four week contract, the director of the program took us out to lunch and offered his congratulations on our success. It seems that we had finally achieved something that the *Summer Arts* crew had been trying to do for some years. We had managed to lure the students into the wonderful world of creative collaboration. Our roles had been to foster cross-genre interaction and we'd taken up the baton and run with it as enthusiastically as any Olympic athlete.

We were proud of our achievements and had sat in the audience the year before watching the student's final presentations like doting parents. We couldn't have been any prouder as 'our' young actors used the emotive scripts that 'our' young writers had created. 'Our' young dancers were accompanied by 'our' young musicians. Our hearts burst with the satisfaction that comes from knowing you have been part of such a rewarding and exciting cultural experience.

We also knew that the university had noticed and recognised our efforts. On one of our final mornings of that first year, as we wandered around the campus, the Dean had drawn us aside and with great pomp and ceremony bestowed an honorary 'masters of intermingling' on both of us. We arrived at the lunch confident that the Director would also express his delight in how the program had gone that year.

As lunch arrived at the table, the Director showered us with compliments and statements of appreciation. He concluded his verbal thank you by asking us to return the following year. 'And we want to double your pay.' He thumped the table as a gesture of emphasis.

Sue-Ellen and I looked at each other; we were both beaming. To come back for another *Summer Arts* was incredibly exciting and, as if rehearsed, we said simultaneously 'Uuummm, let us think about it for a fraction of a second—YES!!!' We sealed the deal by downing the large glasses of chilled water in front of us.

When I left Australia to be part of *Summer Arts* in 2002, we had no idea that Philip had cancer. The 2003 departure saw him flying over with me, which necessitated fine orchestration of the timing for his three monthly hormone injections.

The treatment had just started and, so far, it was deemed too early to undertake any tests to find out if it was working. The immediate side effects had been difficult. The injection is huge and the needle site ached painfully for some days. The impact of suddenly cutting Philip's testosterone levels was understandably intense. He experienced dramatic mood swings and his levels of paranoia in particular were elevated to unbearable proportions.

I developed a deeper understanding and a great empathy for people living with people with brain injuries where behaviour is adversely and unpredictably affected. Within days of the first administration, my calm, gentle Philip had suddenly morphed into a demon. His rages escalated and he compensated by increasing his already significant wine intake as a way to drown the demon that the hormone therapy had set loose inside him. Under the influence of this dreaded cocktail, his moods would swing from sad and depressed to angry and blaming. I was subjected to accusations of causing his cancer, of ignoring him, of deliberately making life difficult for him. He would rant and rave into the early hours of the morning, telling me he resented my professional success and my personal popularity. I knew this behaviour was being fuelled by the injections and the alcohol, but that didn't make dealing with it any easier.

One such night of rages proved to be more than I could tolerate. Philip had consumed the best part of a bottle of red wine on his own. My initial response to his heavy drinking had been to try drinking it myself. My logic was that if I drank the wine then he couldn't and I was therefore, in some ridiculous way, saving him from himself. I quickly realised the stupidity of this approach, especially as he just bought more wine to ensure there was always another bottle. Having woken up to the fact that in trying to save his liver I was systematically destroying my own, I cut back my intake and watched in panic as his continued to rise.

This one particular night, I'd poured myself a glass of wine to have with dinner and Philip determinedly guzzled the rest. He was quite quickly intoxicated and the yelling and abuse started. I was over it! My own wine glass sat on the table in front of me still three-quarters full. I remember I calmly stood up and without uttering a single word, threw the contents in Philip's face, picked up my meal and walked to the kitchen to finish it in peace.

The house was suddenly shrouded in silence—that awkward silence that denotes that something really difficult has just happened and nobody knows what to do. Philip went to the bedroom, washed his face and changed his clothes. Not a word was said. Passing back through the kitchen, he went to the fridge and selected a bottle of champagne. When I saw which bottle he was starting to open, I freaked.

I'd recently been given a bottle of champagne which I knew retailed at about $90 and I was saving it for a special occasion. (Spending that sort of money on a bottle of wine isn't something I would do very often and it seemed like it would be a lovely treat.) There was also a $10 bottle of sparkling wine in the fridge. Philip had taken out the expensive one and was busy taking the foil off so he could get to the cork.

'There's a cheap bottle in the fridge. Have that,' I said. My logic was that, given he was already drunk, the expensive one would be wasted on him anyway.

His temper flared again. 'What, so I'm not worth this champagne? I'm only worth the cheap one, am I?'

I could see there was no point in pursuing this. 'Have what you like,' I spat at him, threw the rest of my dinner in the bin and headed outside to sit on the deck.

I watched as Philip went outside into the darkness. The bottle of champagne had been opened, though he carried no glass from which to drink it. Clearly he wasn't going to bother pouring it into anything other than his throat. He was also carrying a lit hurricane lamp, and he was heading into the bush at the back of our block.

'Great,' I thought, 'Now you're going to write yourself off, pass out, and probably set fire to the property.' I didn't even know until that night that there was a place that was beyond anger, but I had landed there with a painful bump. I saw no point in following him. He was bigger and stronger than I was and in his inebriated state, he was not going to be reasoned with.

From my vantage point on the deck, I watched for any signs of a fire, and when 11.00 pm came and no burning bush had presented itself, I went to bed. I remember lying there feeling totally isolated, unbearably alone and completely distressed. Tears welled up and poured down my face like flood waters over a spillway. I'm amazed at the endless supply of tears that we can cry.

I'm not sure when I fell asleep that night, but I was woken at 2.00 am by the sound of sobbing. Philip had returned and he was out on the deck. He'd lost his glasses, his clothes were covered in mud and dirt (clearly he'd had a number of falls), the hurricane lamp was intact and no longer burning and he was a heaving, sobbing, distraught mess. I went out to him. He was too drunk to talk, but I managed to get him into the house and onto the couch where he immediately passed out. I went back to bed, deciding that tomorrow we were going to discuss a new plan. Fuelled by my own extreme tiredness, I fell back into a fitful sleep.

Philip was drawn and hung over the next morning and profusely apologetic. 'I don't care,' I insisted, 'Whatever is creating this has to be managed'. The next couple of days were tense and I watched as the effects of the hormone treatment lost their momentum and some of the old Philip returned. He spoke of his painful frustration, explaining that he knew what he was doing but was unable to stop himself. As the treatment continued, it became evident that the first two weeks following the injection were by far the worst in terms of mood difficulties. That the emotional oscillation was coupled with the constant pain from the injection site was very difficult; however, I was certain that this destructive cycle couldn't continue.

I urged Philip to get professional help for his anger. I could only see benefits for him if he were to deal with the issues from his past that were clearly very debilitating, but he held firm to this belief that talking wasn't going to help him (we never reached agreement on that one) and instead he decided he was coming to America with me. I'm still not sure how 'see a therapist' evolved into 'book an airfare', but it did. Dr James orchestrated his treatment regime to fit and the bank agreed to extend the mortgage on our home to provide the funds, so we decided to extend the trip to take in England and Europe and be away for the three months between injections.

Dr James also declared that by the time we returned, Philip would have gone through enough complete cycles to justify more tests, which would establish whether the hormone treatment was working or not. We both figured that maybe some time away was just what we needed.

Build up great memories—and
accept the gifts life brings

We flew into Heathrow and spent some time in England catching up with my family. Philip had met them before and it was evident that they liked him. As was normal for him pre-cancer, he was charming, witty and intelligent and as the time wore on and the effects of the hormone treatment stabilised, I saw frequent evidence of the 'lovely Philip' I knew and loved. I remember there were lots of laughs, plenty of sightseeing, and for me to be surrounded by loving family was enormously helpful.

We also included a week in Paris. This was one of our favourite cities and the site of many happy memories for us from our time living very frugally in France a couple of years earlier. We had booked a unit on the Left Bank for the week. It was our first foray into internet travel booking. The unit was considerably smaller than we'd been led to believe (photos are so deceiving), but it was comfortable and well located.

There was one small hiccup. On the plot of land next door, a multi-storey construction was underway. The workers arrived early each morning and started up ear-splitting machinery. Our thoughts of idyllic sleep-ins and long, lazy brunches on the balcony (which was so small it didn't take a chair anyway) were shattered. Instead, we were up with the sun and out into the busy city just to escape the jackhammers. Thankfully, our booking included a weekend and we were blissfully grateful when it became evident that the work crews were taking two days off.

The combination of family time and Paris was just what we both needed, and for a few glorious weeks it felt like we were back on track. Our equilibrium, which had taken such a beating with the impact of the hormone therapy, was being wonderfully restored. Our time was filled with wondrous people and magical places. Having spent significant time in Paris previously, we were both happy to abandon the sightseeing rituals in favour of hanging out on the Left Bank, loitering in coffee shops, sauntering up and down colourful Parisian streets and relaxing over river cruise dinners. When not enjoying the delights of the Seine in the evening, we shopped at local markets and prepared delicious meals in our apartment. It was a gorgeous, laughter-filled time and we both enjoyed what felt to us like a bit of a holiday from cancer.

We flew from Paris to New York. I'd visited New York before with a musician friend and we'd occupied ourselves taking in many of the tourist highlights, with a particular focus on the entertainment quarter. Returning to New York with a political activist saw us undertaking a whole different type of tour, incorporating the United Nations, the High Court and other sites of political significance.

Philip and I had long had a tradition of 'date night'. Each month, we would set aside an evening for a special dinner. We alternated who would organise date night, and being very competitive in nature, we were continuously trying to outdo each other. My turn to organise a date had coincided with our time in Paris and I thought my river dinner cruise on the Seine would be hard to beat. New York was our last stop before I took myself off to

Summer Arts. Philip was planning to fly north to Canada once I headed west to Fresno, so one night out of the blue he declared that date night should be brought forward. He proceeded to whisk me off to a Louisiana-style Cajun restaurant not far from Broadway. We gorged ourselves on jambalaya and were both pleased that a good walk separated us from our hotel. I suspect we waddled back, the toe tapping rhythms of the Deep South still ringing in our ears.

The following morning I flew to Fresno for the *Summer Arts* Festival. Philip headed to Canada, bound for Nova Scotia, where he was planning an ocean kayak adventure. The holiday had done us both good. Philip was looking strong and robust, but appropriately sad, as I waved through the rear window of the taxi that was transporting me to the airport. I was refuelled in terms of energy and ready for a month of culture, fun and work.

Once I'd left, Philip, with another day to fill in New York before heading off, took a wander to the site where John Lennon was shot. Later he recounted how he stood on the spot for some time, in his words, immobilised. His thoughts dwelt on how it would feel to suddenly have life taken from you. Understandably, Philip's diagnosis and subsequent prognosis had resulted in him becoming quite focused on, and curious about, death.

We had plans to meet in Los Angeles in a few weeks time and, on completion of my contract with *Summer Arts*, we would continue our holiday, exploring parts of California before coming home. It felt incredibly sad to be leaving alone the morning I left for Fresno. Philip was mid-cycle with the hormone treatment, which meant that his energy and his disposition were both restored to endearing and delightful levels. I knew the time in Canada would be good for him and I also knew it would be difficult for us to be separated even just for a few weeks.

I arrived at Fresno airport to be greeted by Sue-Ellen and Jim (the director of the *Summer Arts* program). It was like the three musketeers were together again. The whole year that had lapsed between the 2002 event and now melted swiftly away as we reconnected and were reminded about the potential excitement ahead of us. Having been part of one program, Sue-Ellen and I now knew with confidence that the next four weeks would be outstandingly enjoyable. We weren't disappointed.

Once again, Sue-Ellen and I lived on the campus, occupying student accommodation. Once again, we settled in to co-habit for a month. There aren't many friends with whom I would willingly share a small student unit with for that amount of time but Sue-Ellen and I, having worked together extensively, have a strong sense of who each other is. Our routines established in 2002 were quickly restored. Each afternoon around 5.00, as the mercury soared invariably over 100 degrees Fahrenheit, we would retreat to our air conditioned unit for 'beer o'clock' and ceremoniously share a stubby of beer before getting ready for dinner and attendance at whatever evening event was on offer (and every evening was filled with an array of concerts and performances). We were truly in bliss.

A few days after I arrived, Jim's new partner joined him on campus and was duly introduced to Sue-Ellen and me. We hit it off immediately. I remember arriving at the restaurant where we'd arranged to meet Jim and Gretchen for lunch. They were seated in a booth and quickly reorganised themselves to make room for us. Gretchen and I were seated next to each other and

the conversation flowed easily. It was one of those meetings where you feel you've known the person for a long time.

Gretchen and I caught up often. We would frequently bump into each other and take time out to grab a coffee and engage in more chat. The connection quickly became very strong.

Philip would call each day, using Jim's cell phone at a pre-arranged time to ensure Jim and I were co-located for me to get the call. When Gretchen returned to Los Angeles for a few days, she would also call daily, and often Jim would pass the phone over to me so we could have a brief catch-up. It felt like I had a close friend in America, and that was very comforting.

One morning I saw Jim walking across the campus and caught up with him to say hello. 'I'm glad I bumped into you' he said, and handed me his cell phone 'I'm going to be tied up in a meeting all morning so here, you take this. I'm only expecting two calls anyway and they'd both probably prefer to talk to you'. He said it lightly. He seemed genuinely pleased to have facilitated for me the gift of a friendship with Gretchen.

Summer Arts is configured as two x two week master classes. The first group of students complete their two week intensive experience and then depart and make room for the second group. Each class is co-ordinated by one of the university professors aligned to the particular genre; however, the students are actually taught and get to co-perform with recognised professionals in their chosen field. It was a fantastic experience for culture vultures like Sue-Ellen and me as we got to meet award-winning script writers, well-known musicians and highly-acclaimed dancers. The list was long and impressive.

The middle of the festival (between blocks) is celebrated with an elaborate staff and invited guest dinner. The two years that we attended the program, the dinner was held at the property of one of the retired professors from CalState University, a man who continued to strongly support the *Summer Arts* program as a highly valued patron. Bill was an artist of some renown and creativity and his property was, in my opinion, his most impressive work of art. Filled with an array of thought-provoking sculptures (some lovingly created by Bill himself and others gifts of nature that had been expertly showcased) and enshrined in beautiful gardens, the property sat atop a hill and offered breathtaking 360^0 views. It epitomised a level of peace and tranquillity that refused to be captured by photographs and defied even the most skilled wordsmith. It truly was a place that had to be experienced. That I got to experience it twice is a gift that I will be forever thankful for.

On this second visit to *Summer Arts*, we were even more excited about dinner at Bill's than we'd been the year before, because this time we knew what we were about to encounter. Our entourage this year consisted of an eclectic group of artists, and given the ambiance of the place it was only natural that the musicians played, the singers sang, the painters and sculptors sketched and the writers scribbled with gay abandon. Even the most unartistic person would be moved to create something as a result of a few hours at Bill's.

The party was in full swing. There was a small group of us lingering on the lawn, conversation was animated and kept time with the mariachi band playing beside us. It was all upbeat and energised. I recall a gentle breeze starting up and then a sudden stillness.

And the world stopped. I'm not joking or exaggerating.

This sensation had happened to me once before. I was 14 years old and I was at a party up the road from my house. It was a noisy teenage party, lots of yelling, loud music, quite frenetic really, when suddenly a young man in a soldier's uniform appeared in the doorway and the world stopped. Everything went silent and all the people disappeared and I remember feeling scared and overwhelmed. Something big was happening and I had no idea what it was. As quickly as the stillness had descended it lifted, and the party re-materialised and continued as noisily as ever.

Three years later I married that soldier, and even though we are divorced now, our two beautiful daughters and two incredible grandsons are our priceless legacy of the moment that time stood still. Who knows whether the world stopped because I was destined to notice this soldier, or whether I noticed the soldier because the world stopped? That remains a mystery, but the memory is as vivid now as the moment it happened.

And now here I was all these years later, my world and life evolved through immeasurable twists and turns, and whammo! It had happened for a second time.

The mariachi music returned first and then I noticed that all but one of the small group that I'd been chatting with had dispersed and were involved in other conversations. Gretchen stood before me, wine glass poised.

'Wow,' she said and we both knew that we'd had the same experience. 'It must be hard for you at the moment,' she commented. 'Are you worried about Philip being in Canada on his own?'

'Oh, he's pretty independent,' I responded, 'and I have to say he was looking great when I left him in New York. I really think this hormone treatment is working. He is stronger, more vibrant—reconnected somehow. I'll be interested to see what the test results say when we get home. We want to go to India to visit the ashram of Sai Baba, and I think he is well enough to make the journey.'

Sathya Sai Baba was an Indian guru. Some called him an Avatar and I had been intrigued by stories of his 'miracles' and life at his ashram for some years. Ian Gawler talked of his visit to the ashram and his audience with Sai Baba and claimed to have gained much from his time there. Sai Baba's authenticity has been severely questioned in some quarters, but something in me was very keen (almost driven you might say) to experience the ashram for myself. Philip, a 'collapsed Catholic' (a term I've stolen from the character Nancy in Bryce Courtney's *Four Fires*) had always scorned my 'wacky spiritual voodoo stuff', and I was surprised when he suggested one night while we were at the Gawler Centre that we might visit India for the purposes of spending time at Sai Baba's ashram. Whether it was a 'calling' or simply desperation, I don't know, but I resolved then to do my best to make it happen. With Philip's health appearing to be improving, a trip to India seemed possible, and I was excited about the prospect.

I heard Gretchen catch her breath when I mentioned visiting the ashram. 'It's for you!' she said.

'What?' I replied.

'The ash,' she stated firmly, in a voice that suggested I should know what she was talking about. When my facial response clearly indicated I didn't, she went on to explain.

Some years earlier a friend of hers had gone to visit Sai Baba and had managed to get an audience with him. Sai Baba had 'produced' some of the famous *vibhutti* in front of him. (It was reported by many that they witnessed Sai Baba create this white ash out of nothing. It just appeared in his hands.) He packaged it up. When handing the package over he stated, 'This is not for you, you will pass it on. It isn't for that person either; the person you pass it on to will know what to do with it. They will meet someone that they need to pass it on to. In this way, it will get to the correct person. Everybody will know when and to whom to pass it; don't try to work it out, just go with the message when it comes.'

Her friend brought the *vibhutti* home and held on to it for some time until one day Gretchen was visiting him and he said he had a strong feeling that he should give it to her. He said that her role was to pass it on and she would know when. Since then, she said she had met many people who might have been valid recipients of the *vibhutti* but never had she felt the message to pass it on until tonight. 'The *vibhutti* is for Philip,' she stated without hesitation. 'I feel it so strongly; I know it is true.'

The little package of *vibhutti* was transferred to me a few days later, and subsequently passed onto Philip who religiously ended his shower ritual every morning by placing some in his navel. (His reason for this was that he believed he had received a message in a dream to use it in this way.) We both took the appearance of the 'magic ash' and the way that it had come to us as a sign. The trip to India eventuated the following year.

Live! Because in the midst of life ...

My next *Summer Arts* story relates to yet another 'T-bar with death'. On the third weekend of the festival, Philip was flying from Canada to Los Angeles. I planned to meet him in LA, where we had organised to hire a Mustang convertible. Philip and I would travel back to Fresno together, spend a few days there so he could meet the crew I worked with, and then he would go on to some sightseeing on his own. On the completion of my contract, he would return to pick me up and we'd spend a couple of weeks driving round California before flying home to Brisbane. I was excited about seeing Philip again and looking forward to our planned adventure.

In preparation to go to meet him, I'd commandeered one of the computers in the *Summer Arts* office for the purposes of booking a hotel in LA for the night of his arrival. One of the office staff kindly offered to give me a hand.

Every hotel I found on Wotif.com was summarily dismissed. They were all located in areas deemed 'too dangerous'.

'Are there any safe areas in LA?' I asked teasingly, for surely my advisor was being over cautious.

'Not many', she replied. 'You sure you want to go?'

'Of course I'm sure,' I returned as I pushed myself away from the computer screen and handed her my visa card. 'Here, you book something, that way you'll feel more comfortable about me going.'

She settled on Marina del Rey and located a comfortable looking hotel at a reasonable price. 'It's pretty close to the airport,' she said. 'Whatever you do, don't go downtown, especially at night. We'll never see you again if you do'.

I had also heard about the dangers of 'downtown', although I suspected that she was adding some spice to the story. I resolved to heed her advice.

The next challenge was how to get there. When travelling overseas, I love taking local public transport, but this idea was immediately canned by Jim. 'You have to be joking!' he exclaimed, clearly questioning my sanity. 'Take my car. That's an order.'

I've never been one to be ordered and anyway, Philip and I were picking up the hire car in LA and I didn't see the point in us driving back separately. Philip was keen to come to *Summer Arts* and I wanted him to meet everybody so, in my mind, however I got to LA, it would not be by me driving.

Seeing my determination, Jim organised a compromise, 'Gretchen's going back to LA. She will drive you,' he announced. 'You two will enjoy the drive together, I'm sure.'

Gretchen drove me to the outskirts of LA and then true to my traveller spirit I resolved to negotiate the bus system to Marina del Rey. After all, what could possibly go wrong?

The bus timetables were readily available at the library, so I had Gretchen drop me off at one of them and I proceeded to arm myself with the necessary brochures and timetables and set off in a determined way for the bus stop.

The first bus came right on time and the driver was very helpful (as I have found most Americans to be). We travelled for some one and a half hours and then he pulled over just near Chinatown and advised me which bus I was looking out for, pointing out the bus stop on the other side of the road.

A small group of people were waiting at the bus stop, so I made my way over and was very quickly engaged in 'travel talk 101'. ('Where are you from? What do you think of the States? Is Brisbane near Sydney?' etc. etc.) The conversation was fun, though the absence of a bus was disconcerting.

'Shouldn't the bus have arrived by now?' I enquired of my new fellow travellers in waiting.

'Yes, it's very late. I'll ring and see what's happening'.

It turned out that there had been an incident at the bus depot and the buses were blocked in. The bus service had temporarily ceased while transport workers endeavoured to move the broken down bus that was holding everybody in the yard. My new friend advised that it was expected that there could be another half hour delay and then the bus would come.

What I love about travel is the potential absence of time-related stress. In this instance, I had hours. Philip's plane wasn't due in until that evening and I had no particular need to be arriving at my hotel imminently. In fact I was rather enjoying this delay, so I resumed the conversation and resolved to chill out.

The suggested 30 minutes well past, my new friends started to drift away, leaving me alone at the bus stop. No problems, there were plenty of people around. It all felt pretty good, and I was confident that any second the bus I was waiting for would materialise.

Then I noticed that almost all the people had disappeared, and the street, which had been bustling with people a few minutes ago, was suddenly almost empty. My attention drifted to two men lingering on the corner just over from me, where a transaction that appeared to resemble a drug deal (an assessment I made having been well educated in these matters by movies and television shows) was taking place. I shifted my gaze so as not to get involved, and then both men disappeared.

It was eerie. The busy street of just a short while ago was now deserted. I began to feel very anxious and dedicated all my focus to the energy of the universe to please, quickly send me a solution.

And then I received an unforgettable reminder that, at any time, death might only be just seconds away. A large Cadillac came gliding down the street. Moving very slowly, it all felt very Al Capone-like, and suddenly the whole scene took on a surreal energy. I watched, horrified, as the car approached me. All my senses were on hyper alert; I just knew that this situation wasn't good. The sound of automatic gun fire exploded in my brain. As the car moved past a group of cars parked directly across the road from me, two occupants opened fire and blasted the parked cars. Panic doesn't describe my reaction. The only reason I was still standing was because the gunmen fired out to their left. Had they had turned to their right, I would have been gunned down.

I re-sent my plea to the heavens to send help and literally within seconds, a taxi screeched to a halt in front of me. The back door of the taxi swung open and revealed the biggest man I have ever seen. This man took up the entire bench seat across the front of the car and his head was bent on an obscure angle so as to fit his height into the car. I promise I am not exaggerating.

'Get in!' the driver demanded, and in a state of complete shock, I did.

'What are you doing here?' his voice vibrated with horror. 'Nobody comes here after dark. NOBODY!' At that point, I noticed that the sun had sunk and day was turning into night.

My reply sounded inane to my own ears, and my voice had taken on the quality and timbre of a five year old. 'I'm waiting for a bus.' Every part of me was shaking.

'I would never normally come down this street, none of us EVER comes down this street after dark,' continued my giant of a rescuer, 'but I was passing the intersection up there and I felt compelled to take the turn. Thank God I did, because if you had stayed here you wouldn't have seen the morning. Where are you going?'

I gave him the address of the hotel and he accelerated away at break neck speed. Even in my terror, I was struck by the irony of surviving a drive-by shooting only to get killed in the getaway taxi.

We arrived safely at Marina del Rey. When the taxi driver dropped me off, he emphasised again, 'Don't go downtown at night, EVER, do you hear me?'

My five year old voice still in operation, I mumbled something that sounded like a promise not to, tipped him handsomely and stumbled to the reception. I was very relieved when I found some wine in the fridge of the hotel room and delirious with excitement when a few hours later Philip burst excitedly and glowing with health through the door.

'How was your trip from Fresno?' he asked.

'You'll never believe it,' I responded. 'Want a drink?'

Death hovers around us constantly and reminds us just how fragile we are.

The following quote from *The Tibetan Book of Living and Dying* sums it up for me:

> *Why is it so very hard to practice death and to practice freedom? And why exactly are we so frightened of death that we avoid looking at it altogether? Somewhere, deep down, we know we cannot avoid facing death forever. We know, in Milarepa's words, "This thing called 'corpse' we dread so much is living with us here and now." The longer we postpone facing death, the more we ignore it, the greater the fear and insecurity that build up to haunt us. The more we try to run away from that fear, the more monstrous it becomes.*

I don't know whether or not I had a close call that night in LA. Al Capone didn't seem to be after me and I suspect I was just an unwilling witness to a random event. However, once again, as with the building collapse and the motorcycle accident outside our house, death had glided past me and left yet another scratch. I could feel it stinging painfully.

Draw strength from nature's beauty

Philip's beaming good health was immediately noticed when we got to the campus at Fresno. Sue-Ellen couldn't believe how well he looked, particularly in comparison to how he had been just a couple of weeks earlier when she'd caught up with us in Brisbane.

Jim commented to me afterwards that after hearing the accounts of Philip's health, he had prepared himself to greet a frail, ill man and was delighted when Philip leapt from the car and strode purposefully across the car park, hand outstretched to greet him.

I hadn't seen Philip look so well for years, and it confirmed for me that his cancer had been impacting on him for some time. (From far before we started any interactions with doctors, I believe.) It was wonderful to be able to show him around the campus. He attended some performances with us and shared lots of meals and conversations with the *Summer Arts* crew.

All too soon, we were saying good bye again as he loaded up the Mustang and took off. He was headed for San Francisco and from there he planned to follow Highway One back to LA. He would then loop back to Fresno and pick me up and we'd head off together for some serious national park, mountain and desert exploration.

He duly returned just over a week later, still looking strong and healthy. It was easy to slip into an illusion that the hormone treatment had worked a miracle. One thing Dr James had been specific about was that the hormone treatment wasn't a cure. With Phillip's cancer as advanced as it was, the best we could hope for from the quarterly injections was what was termed 'a biochemical remission'. This meant that the injections could hold, slow down and possibly even reverse the cancer slightly; however, it was almost impossible that it would eradicate it all together.

I am a firm believer in miracles and a chronic sceptic of 'impossible', so I allowed myself the luxury of speculating that Philip would defy all the research (after all, people did that all the time) and that the hormone treatment would cast the cancer from his body.

It was the relaxed, energetic, fun-loving Philip I'd originally fallen in love with who joined me on that driving holiday of California. Our first stop after leaving the Fresno campus was Yosemite National Park.

Sue-Ellen and I had visited Yosemite a couple of times the year before. The first time was with a visiting world class chamber music orchestra who were part of the *Summer Arts* team in 2002. We were the musical equivalent of international sporting 'orange girls'. Our role was to accompany the group and ensure that refreshments were made available, thus enabling the musicians to focus on their roles as mentors to the students and masters of their craft.

I remember watching, mesmerised, as the violins were carefully unpacked and the centuries-old cello taken lovingly from its case. My ears delighted in the ritual of tuning and synchronising and then finally the first notes rang out across the canyon. I still tingle with privilege as I remember that day—the haunting sound of the strings, the vivid blue sky, the smell of the giant sequoias and the unsurpassable acoustics of nature. What a truly remarkable place for a concert. The soothing sounds of ancient scores drifted across the park, each note brushing gently past each blade of grass, and I sensed that even the wildlife stood transfixed in auditory awe.

The repertoire complete, we shared sandwiches and easy flowing conversation. There are so many moments in life that feel perfect. That first visit to Yosemite was very much one of those moments for me.

Sue-Ellen and I returned a few weeks later, this time with hiking boots rather than musicians, and explored some of the trails and vistas. I had fallen in love with Yosemite that first year that Sue-Ellen and I had ventured there—so much so that upon completion of the 2002 contract, I had signed up for a back packers tour and run away to Yosemite for three days of delicious camping and hiking. Jim expressed great concern to Sue-Ellen when he heard.

'She's going camping with strangers!' he exclaimed in a conversation they were having.

'She does it all the time,' Sue-Ellen confirmed. 'She'll be fine'.

Returning in 2003, I was filled with excitement and anticipation. I knew I could never get enough of the peaceful grandeur of this amazing natural treasure.

As we prepared to leave the Fresno campus at the completion of the 2003 *Summer Arts*, Philip positioned himself in the driver's seat, looked over at me, winked cheekily and enquired, 'where to, then?'

'Yosemite,' I replied without hesitation and a nostalgic wave of exhilaration swept through me.

We hit the road. Philip had clearly adjusted to driving on the other side of the road as he was confident and poised behind the wheel. He also seemed to be very at home with the power of the Mustang, and I wondered how many speeding tickets he might have accumulated in his travels thus far.

'So what makes Yosemite so special?' His question broke the silence and brought my attention back to the car.

'Too hard to describe,' I answered, 'you'll have to wait and see'.

Coming from Fresno, you approach Yosemite via a long tunnel. When you enter the tunnel for the first time, you are unprepared for what awaits you as you exit the other end. My first time through this tunnel is still burnt into my brain. It all seemed ordinary at first. The scenery as you approach is quite pleasant and the drive to get there is certainly enjoyable, offering well-made roads all clearly signed. I always found the trip to Yosemite to be quite easy and relaxed. You enter the tunnel with few expectations, or at least I had on my first visit, so the experience of exiting was quite literally breathtaking.

Philip had sat back in his seat and was looking confident and relaxed. The trip so far had certainly done him the world of good and I was pleased that we had decided that he would accompany me. A hint of blue alerted me that we were about to exit the tunnel. 'Get ready,' I warned and then we burst forth from the darkness and were faced with the awe-inspiring vista of the canyon. Nature had heralded our arrival at Yosemite in the most spectacular of ways.

Philip's gasp was audible, as I suspect everybody's is the first time they exit the darkness and emerge into the splendour of this natural phenomenon. The surging momentum of the glacier that had, all those eons ago, carved its way through the rock to form the basin that is Yosemite is evident. It's impossible not to be touched by the obvious power of nature so sensationally juxtaposed beside the gentle beauty of the ancient flora.

This one noble park is big enough and rich enough for a whole life of study and aesthetic enjoyment. It is good for everybody, no matter how benumbed with care, encrusted with a mail of business habits like a tree with bark. None can escape its charms. Its natural beauty cleans and warms like a fire, and you will be willing to stay forever in one place like a tree.

John of the Mountains: The Unpublished Journals of John Muir, (1938).

Philip was as taken with Yosemite as I was and we ambled and sauntered for hours. We lunched at the magnificent Ahwahnee dining room, a truly memorable gastronomic experience, gazed in admiration at the intrepid climbers scaling the sheer face of El Capitan and sat memorised for what seemed like hours watching a young bear cub playing in a lake (ensuring we stayed quite some distance away and on constant lookout for mum, of course). It was a hot, dry day, yet despite the soaring temperatures we skipped playfully along the trails.

Around mid-afternoon, we started to make our way north towards Lake Tahoe. Given the heat of the day, we decided to close the roof of the car and set the climate control. Still dressed for our afternoon ambles, we were wearing shorts and tee-shirts. The road out was steep, really steep. The altitude rose quickly and, unbeknownst to us in our climate-controlled comfort, the temperatures plummeted, a fact that only became evident when we noticed specks of what appeared to be snow on the side of the road. I'm not kidding. Snow!

The higher we got, the more substantial the snow patches became, gradually joining up to become small snow drifts. As we continued the snow got deeper, until we found ourselves driving behind the snow plough. It was amazing. Just a few hours before we had been literally sweltering in 100+ degrees (Fahrenheit) and now it was snowing. Philip, a born and bred Queenslander, was overcome with excitement. He had only seen snow a few times in his life and he wasn't missing out on the experience. He pulled the car over and before I got a chance to say 'jacket', he was out and running through the snow in shorts and sandals. Needless to say, it was a rather quick sprint before he was back, lamenting breathlessly, 'It's bloody cold out there!'

We'd gone to California in summer. Neither of us had thought to pack snow gear! We did the best we could with the light jackets we had and arriving at the next small town found ourselves a motel for the night. The following morning I sat comfortably in the heated dining room enjoying breakfast, when a fluttering movement outside the window caught my attention. There was the most beautiful, delicate little hummingbird busily extracting pollen from the colourful tree blossoms. As I'd sat enchanted by the bear cub the day before, so I sat there now, mesmerised by the hummingbird.

Over the next few days, we looped our way back down south. Philip was determined to visit Death Valley and exclaimed his excitement as we passed through the gates to the National Park. We were back into excessively hot weather and the valley was dry. Being summer, it wasn't high tourist season (due to the high temperatures) and the memory of Yosemite seemed like a cool change. The car registered temperatures over 120 degrees (again Fahrenheit) and locals warned us that it could get much higher than that. Signs everywhere warned that visitors must carry water and warnings at the start of all the trails advised that once you have drunk half the water you are carrying, you MUST turn back.

It was dry and almost desolate, yet intriguing and somehow relaxing. The motel where we stayed was a cool oasis and provided a wonderful evening retreat. That the barman mixed one of the best margaritas that I'd ever tasted was just a fantastic bonus, really.

On our final day in Death Valley we headed off in a new direction, intent on just wandering aimlessly (our favourite way to travel). We'd just drive until we came to somewhere that took our attention, at which point we'd get out of the car and walk until we couldn't cope with the heat anymore. Then we'd drive on, enjoying the air conditioning of the Mustang, until we found somewhere else to explore. There was no plan, no timeframe, no anything really—just pure, unadulterated freedom. As the afternoon started to close on this particular day, our attention was drawn to the rapidly gathering clouds. As they gathered, they darkened. In anybody's language they were spelling rain. When the heavens opened, it was to provide a deluge of momentous proportions. The rain bucketed down. Visibility was instantly reduced to almost nothing. Queensland often impresses with her storms, and this one more than matched any our home state had ever produced. To describe it I need terms that go beyond 'torrential' and 'cyclonic', as they just don't cut it for this experience. As quickly as the rain had started, it suddenly stopped. The storm, torrid and intense as it had been, was over in less than five minutes. Having pulled over to await its passing, Philip pulled back out on the road and we continued our way back to the motel.

About 10 minutes later, we passed a car full of young men. The passengers were hanging out the window yelling something as they passed. We concluded that they were just mucking around and didn't take much notice. We were still discussing the impressive meteorological performance that we'd witnessed when we turned a corner and there before us, rather than the road we were expecting, was a giant heap of rocks and rubble. That five minute storm had managed to spark a massive landslide, completely cutting off our only access to the motel that was to be our haven for the night (not to mention those magnificent margaritas).

Philip was never one to be daunted by things like landslides and much to my horror and amazement he selected first gear and started to move the sports car forward. We hadn't gone far when we were met head on by a ranger who flashed the lights of his Hummer at us and waved us to stop.

He approached the car with an amused grin. 'Where are you from, stranger?' His smile revealed his awareness that we had to be tourists. Clearly locals would never try anything this stupid.

'Australia,' Philip met his grin with one of his own.

'You won't get through. 'I've barely made it in that,' he nodded towards the Hummer. 'You're going to have to turn back, I'm afraid'.

'Any way we can get around?' Philip asked, conceding.

'Sure is,' came the instant reply. 'You'll need to go back the way you came, cross the border into Nevada and then come around and back through the other side. It'll take you a few hours, but it's a nice drive'.

It was a long trip back to our accommodation and neither of us felt like a margarita when we finally arrived, exhausted but content. We hadn't planned to visit Nevada and I certainly wouldn't profess to have seen much of it, but it was another adventure for us. With Philip doing so well, we were up for as many adventures as we could get.

*Fly high when you can—and
grieve for those who can't*

The hormone treatment was working! We were gathered excitedly in Dr James' office. The PSA had dropped to single figures. We were ecstatic. Dr James had completely lost control of himself and was looking Philip straight in the face, his own face displaying a broad, beaming smile.

'These are great results, Philip, I'm very happy.'

'Take a back seat, Doc,' replied Philip. I could feel that he was literally shaking with relief. 'You can't possibly be happier than me.'

Dr James declined to engage in a competition about who was happier, opting instead to return to the test results to confirm the good news they held.

'So,' started Philip. 'Does this mean I can look forward to a long life?'

'I've no idea,' stated Dr James. He appeared to be trying to be serious, but his smile betrayed him and he went on to jokingly comment, 'You might get hit by a bus when you walk out of here. All I know is that these results are good, and naturally I'm recommending we keep going with the hormone injections.'

For one delirious moment I forgot the rages and the outbursts. With results like these, we were definitely going to keep going with the hormone treatment.

Dr James presented us with a further prescription, reiterated that he was happy for our GP or a proficient nurse if we knew one to administer the drug, wrote out a request for a further PSA check in three months time, and sent us on our way.

We skipped across the car park. A lightness had overcome both of us that had me thinking that if we weren't careful, we could suddenly take off Mary Poppins-style, but without the umbrella. We headed off to Park Road (one of the popular cafe strips in Brisbane) and ordered celebratory lunches.

We were back on allied territory, having crossed an exhausting and harsh battlefield, and we were overjoyed.

Philip (now a collapsed vegan) lashed out with a steak and a full-bodied red wine. He chatted with the waiter as his meal and drink were brought to him. As the waiter returned to the kitchen, Philip looked across at me and announced 'I want to fly.' I realised that he hadn't completely lost his senses when he went on to explain that he had decided to fulfil a long held childhood dream to get his pilot's licence.

'Oh, so you mean in a plane,' I responded, relieved that our next search wasn't going to be for a set of wings for him.

Our meal continued with an air of safety that was comforting and wonderfully enjoyable. The death sentence that the urologist had predicted had lifted, and with the recent tests results, so were we. We lingered over the meal, neither of us in any rush to leave the social atmosphere of Park Road.

Clearly, our luck was changing because as well the great test results, that week a rather lucrative joint workshop contract landed in our lap. Philip was still struggling to get his consultancy business off the ground. Bits and pieces of work were coming in, but nothing regular or reliable. By contrast, I was flat out with workshops booked almost every day. Evenings and weekends were consumed with workbook development and office accounts.

The money was coming in steadily and going out at an almost equal rate as medical expenses continued to escalate. Further, we were deep in plans for India, and somehow I needed to find the money for us both to travel and for us to survive the planned six weeks of our absence without income. When those who are self-employed don't work, they don't earn.

A few days after the great PSA results, with me pondering how we could raise the additional money for India and flying lessons, a regular client contacted me and invited me to meet with him to discuss some issues in his organisation. Essentially, as is often the case, the issues were all stemming from some systemic communication problems. Philip's forte as a professional negotiator was to manage such situations of sensitive conflict, and as his presentation skills were well-honed, I had no hesitation working up a proposal for a series of workshops that we would co-facilitate. The resulting income would fund our India trip and cover expenses during our absence, so the contract felt very well timed. I also hoped that it would serve to re-build Philip's professional self-esteem, which had taken a hiding through the lack of consultancy work under his own name.

The proposal accepted, we set about developing the workshops. Philip was also researching options for gaining a pilot's licence and I was guardedly enthusiastic, as I wasn't sure how we were going to pay for the additional expense of lessons. Philip had a saying that 'if money is your only problem then you don't have any problems'.

By contrast, I have a tendency to be over-cautious with money as, in the aftermath of my divorce, I'd known a terrifying lack of it. At times I had no way of feeding my children other than through the generous donations of meals from friends—acts of kindness that I will never forget. Further, I was finding it difficult to manage the role of 'What If Mint' that Philip had allocated to me. I stayed quiet about the flying lessons. I loved the idea of him fulfilling his dream, but I was scared about how I'd raise the money to fund it. I was very conscious that we still had a long medical road ahead. That road sucks up savings like there is no tomorrow.

We launched ourselves into the workshops enthusiastically. Philip seemed to enjoy being back at work, and I believe we made an impressive team in the training room. The groups were responsive and the workshops went very well. I was aware that Philip's personality type, whilst highly competent in the face to face world of work that we were professionally inhabiting, would result in him being very drained by the end of the day. I, on the other hand, am highly energised by such work so I would end each day on a high. One day, though, he was different. It didn't seem like work related tiredness. He was distracted, and I felt a fragility about him that I hadn't witnessed since the great PSA results.

I was terrified that the cancer was launching a new assault and that, by encouraging him back to work, I had somehow contributed to it happening. At the end of the day in question, Philip was looking particularly tired and, realising that he was going to find it difficult to hold out for dinner until we got home and had time to prepare something, we decided to stop for an Indian meal. He was pensive and withdrawn in the restaurant and I desperately searched for conversation.

By some fluke of fate, I instigated a conversation about a couple we had met at the Gawler Centre. The woman, a young mother with four children under eight, had advanced breast cancer. She had spoken emotively in her introduction about her fears around leaving her babies motherless, and she tugged at all our heartstrings when she described her anguish about coming away to the retreat without them for ten whole days, knowing that her time with her family might be very limited.

I had attended the support person sessions with her husband and he had spoken at length about his own terror that his beautiful wife might die soon—and his fear that he wouldn't be able to raise their children alone. He was a man in deep panic and I felt for him deeply.

The family had planned a trip to Queensland and we had invited them to come and stay with us. I had suddenly remembered that the time of their planned visit was imminent and this had caused me to think about them a few times during the day. Bringing them into our dinner conversation seemed natural and I hoped it would return Philip from wherever he had emotionally run away to.

'They should be here soon.' I was aware that I was gibbering on a bit, but I noticed that Philip instantly froze, fork lifted between plate and mouth. I saw the corner of his mouth quiver.

'What is it?' I enquired quietly, seeing Philip's distress but not making connections.

The fork stayed mid-air as if even it couldn't work out what to do. Philip kept making funny gurgling noises. He was staring at me, tears had started to slide down his cheeks, and his lips were moving but no words were discernible. I reached for the fork and placed it back on his plate, returning my hand to his to hold it. In a blinding flash, I suddenly knew what was coming and I felt my own capacity for speech disappear as well. Philip found the words first. 'She died,' he blurted, like it couldn't be true and even if it was, it felt like his voice was betraying her by saying it. I went cold.

'What?' I was mystified. There was talk at Gawler about dying (lots of talk) and we all knew that there would be casualties— that same level of knowing that soldiers must carry to war— but the knowing and reality can be opposing forces facing off against each other.

'When?' was my next question.

Another one of the Gawler participants had established an email contact list and had done a remarkable job of keeping news circulating right up until she lost her own battle with kidney cancer. An email had come from her a few days earlier with the tragic news that this young mother's biggest fear had been realised. Her four tiny children would grow up without their glorious mother.

Philip hadn't mentioned the email to me at all. 'I couldn't,' he explained. 'It hurt so much and I didn't want you to hurt. This is the reality, isn't it, some of us, many of us are going to die. All those people who we spent time with, lots of them won't make it—I might not make it. It's too hard, too confronting, I couldn't hear it and I didn't want you to hear it. If I didn't say it then we didn't have to hear it.'

The curry had lost its flavour. We paid the bill and headed home. Rosie and Harry greeted us with leaps of delight. Were they aware of our sadness? They seemed hell bent on cheering us up, though that night we didn't want to be cheered up. Surely everybody is important enough that they deserve for us to feel sadness when they leave us. We are all worthy of people's tears.

We all know that tears won't bring people back. I cried anyway, because tears can help to bring *us* back. They are part of the healing and part of the memories.

That night after we got home from the Indian restaurant, we cried together for the beautiful soul that the world had lost. We cried for her children, some so young they would not carry a personal memory of their mother with them. We cried again for the young woman taken the previous year with bone cancer and we cried for our own fears because even with the 'bio-chemical remission', we knew that we were not out of the woods by a long shot. Dr James had also been clear about that.

The next morning, Philip booked his first flying lesson.

Follow your dreams (even if they include donkeys)

Philip took to flying like an independent eagle whose mother had pushed him out of the nest. He had recently read Richard Bach's *Running from Safety*. The book tells the story of adult Richard returning to meet his child self, Dickie. In the cockpit of a plane, a range of conversations between child and adult take place and Richard reconnects with and re-finds himself through the chats and interactions he has with his child self. Philip was obsessed with this concept of what he would want to tell 'little Phil' from his current perspective as a grown man. What advice, what insights, what warnings, what reassurances would he offer? The book became one of Philip's favourites and I often wonder how much of his time in the cockpit Philip devoted to 'little Phil'.

For myself, I was doing my own flying, mostly in the saddle on the back of a large chestnut thoroughbred called Rocky. I was fulfilling my own dreams to fly without wings and was enjoying my adventure into show jumping and cross-country riding. Wednesday nights became sacrosanct. They were my nights with horses and I guarded them as fiercely as any protective hen might guard her new chicks.

Work continued to boom, which was both a great distraction and a fantastic financial reassurance. My consultancy business was thriving and attracting lucrative contracts. Consequently, I was engaging in lots of travel around and beyond Queensland, which meant I was frequently dashing out to the airport or dashing home from the airport. Life was full and busy and Philip continued to respond well to the hormone treatment.

With Philip also committed to the dream of a small farm, we continued our discussions about the acquisition of more animals, and three alpacas joined our family. (This was a dream inspired by my first viewing of the movie *Dr Dolittle* many years previously.) My cousin Adrian (a constant and wonderful source of support for me despite his being a whole globe away in England) was over visiting for a holiday and he and Philip, along with a mate of Philip's, built the Taj Mahal of barns to accommodate our new arrivals.

Harry and Rosie acted as proficient project supervisors, working side by side with the men and watching with excitement as the project progressed. On completion of the barn (literally just hours before the alpacas arrived), I went down and snapped a photo of the entire construction crew relaxing in the newly completed structure. Harry and Rosie had taken up pride of place, front and centre, and clearly had claimed these salubrious surroundings as their own, looking down on their rather serviceable kennel (complete with verandah) with the sort of level of distaste one might reserve for the view of a slum when seen from the window of a five star hotel. When they were evicted to allow Duncan, Renoir and Chevalier to take up residence, they were not pleased.

Next on our list of desired arrivals were donkeys. They proved slightly more difficult to find and, as with many things in my life, their finding of us was quite a story.

I attended a workshop in Sydney. As part of my own professional development, I attend regular workshops. This one, presented by the Institute of HeartMath, was particularly insightful and fascinating (check them out at www.HeartMath.org.au). A fellow participant was an older woman who hailed from northern NSW, where she ran an alternate healing retreat. She mentioned in a conversation that she had once had donkeys. My ears pricked up: a donkey person! Clearly, I needed to talk to her.

Yes, she confirmed, she had had some donkeys, though they had all died in time and she felt she was too old to get more now.

'I'd love some donkeys,' I said. 'Do you know where I might get some?'

I was delighted when she said immediately that she did and I could barely contain myself when she announced that said donkeys were just round the corner from where I lived. 'Cashmere's in the Samford Valley isn't it, near Clear Mountain?' she asked.

'Yep, I'm right at the base of Clear Mountain,' I replied.

She went on to explain that a naturopath who sometimes offered sessions at her retreat had donkeys—five of them—that he wanted to re-house. That he was literally just up the road from me such a bonus.

I rang said naturopath when I got home but was disappointedly returned to reality when he explained that his five donkeys were all unhandled jacks (intact males). They had been brought down from the wild herds in Central Australia to be dog food and he had outbid the dogger as a way of saving them. They had resided in his paddock ever since. They were maturing into noisy, feisty adolescents, intent on fighting and screaming out for girlfriends. 'My wife is about to leave me and the neighbours want to evict me,' he pleaded. 'I have to find new homes for them.'

Somehow my fantasy of cuddly, friendly, rideable donkeys wasn't matching up to the riotous, deafening behaviour being explained to me, so I politely declined his offer to save his marriage and appease his neighbours and decided to keep looking.

Wednesday night rolled by and I went horse riding.

When I returned, Philip mentioned that a friend had rung and could I ring her back. 'We had quite a chat,' he went on. 'In fact, I asked her about donkeys, because I remembered that her daughter is into horses and I know they aren't necessarily connected but I thought it was worth a go.'

On the mention of donkeys, the friend had immediately advised that her daughter's services wouldn't be required as she herself had a friend with donkeys, a naturopath it seems, and she offered to call him to enquire if he had, or knew of, any loveable longears for re-housing.

The idea that there were two naturopaths with donkeys seemed a bit unbelievable, so assuming we were talking about the same man, I successfully stifled any excitement with regard to donkey additions and returned her call.

No, it turned out, it was a different naturopath. Donkey owner number two didn't have any for sale, but he had offered the name and phone number of a donkey refuge and suggested I ring there.

I was on a roll now so I rang and yes, said the female voice, she could get me some donkeys. She knew of some lovely donkeys, and as luck would have it they were near me.

The circle completed, we trudged up to the top of Clear Mountain and met Jesus and Eeyore. They were two totally wild, intact male donkeys and in a never-regretted moment of complete insanity, I bought them.

The purchase price was relatively cheap, but by the time they arrived at their new home in our paddock they had cost thousands of dollars. I engaged a local horse trainer to transport them, got the vet out and had them gelded, funded a week of training, and on my birthday, the float arrived with my new friends.

Jesus hadn't done well with the castration and on his first night home bled badly, necessitating another vet's visit and few more hundred dollars. The vet treated the wound and administered painkillers and a coagulant. He also gave me his personal mobile phone number and told me he was staying the night up the road and to call him if anything looked worse.

Early the following morning he rang me. 'How's the donkey?' he enquired.

'Fine,' I replied. "He is eating breakfast and there is no indication of any further bleeding.'

'Lives up to his name, hey?' said the vet. 'I really didn't think he would see the sunrise, that one. I was sure he'd die overnight. Well done.'

I put the phone down and said to Philip, 'We've just had our own private Easter. It seems Jesus rose from the dead last night.'

Friends were bemused by my obsession with asses. 'Why donkeys?' they would cry.

'Go and meet them, and you will see,' I urged. Sure enough, they would return from the donkey paddock total converts. Donkeys are loving, generous, kind and intelligent animals. Jesus and Eeyore were to become special friends and they cemented my love of these creatures to the extent that I cannot imagine life without donkeys to play with.

The farm was complete and Philip's treatment was going well, but we weren't going to be given much of break. Sometimes it can feel like every corner holds another challenge. This time, it had my name on it.

Breathe ... just breathe

Despite extensive experience in talking to doctors, it amazes me how difficult it can sometimes be to find something to say. I was face down on the table and my GP was cutting determinedly into my left shoulder. I'd decided it was finally time to get a sebaceous cyst removed. It was nothing serious, but it was very annoying located directly underneath my bra strap, it had developed an annoying habit of flaring up without warning and creating some quite significant pain, especially when I was writing on a whiteboard. Something I do with great regularity as part of my profession. The pain had finally gotten to me and I made an appointment to get it cut out. It was just a routine procedure; nothing to be concerned about.

The GP was engaging in small talk. I couldn't think of much to say, so in response to her question of 'How are things going?' I recounted that I'd been experiencing what I had concluded were just some meaningless symptoms of menopause.

'Uumm,' her voice took on a serious tone. 'We take that stuff pretty seriously'.

The cyst removal over, I sat with her in her consulting rooms.

'I want you to get some tests,' she said as she completed the relevant paperwork. 'It's probably nothing, but it needs to be checked out.'

I assumed the whole thing was a formality; however, I took her advice and a few days later I booked an appointment to have an ultrasound.

Nothing about the situation concerned me. I assumed that the GP was fulfilling her duty of care to ensure that any irregularity was checked out, and it never really occurred to me that anything could be wrong. After all lightning doesn't strike twice—right?

I was pretty slack getting back to the doctor for the results, but did eventually remember to ring. 'Oh yes,' she commented, 'those results are in. Just a minute; I'll go have a look at them.'

Her tone had changed when she came back to the phone. 'I want you to see a gynaecologist.' Her voice was insistent but not panicky.

'What?' I asked. 'Is there a problem?'

'I'm not happy with the ultrasound results. I'm assuming you'd prefer a woman. I'll leave a referral at the front desk. Make an appointment for as soon as you can. Joan, this is important rather than urgent, and it really does need to be done.'

I might have completely panicked, except we knew her response to something really scary. If she had been really worried, she would have made the appointment herself. The fact that she left that up to me indicated that things weren't as frightening as Philip's situation. That said, she had been pretty emphatic on the phone, so the next time I passed the surgery, I collected the referral and made the appointment.

Philip and I waited in the gynaecologist's waiting room in silence. I flicked through magazines. It all felt too familiar. The scene was the same, but the roles had been reserved. When my name was called, I looked up to see a woman of generous proportions beaming at me. I warmed to her instantly. Her smile was contagious and she had an air of confidence that was instantly passed on to me. Philip stood up to come in with me. 'I'd like to just see Joan first,' said Dr Caron. 'But you can come in soon.' Any upsetting reminders of our initial visit to the urologist that might have been sparked by the first part of her response were immediately addressed by the conclusion of the sentence and the relaxed, friendly tone with which she had responded.

Entering her rooms, I was suddenly overcome with anxiety. Interestingly, I'd been pretty calm until that moment, but suddenly the whole ridiculous scenario got the better of me and I started to shake.

'You'll have to excuse me.' My voice held a distinct sound of panic. 'I may overreact; it's just that Philip, my partner, has cancer, so we're a bit super-sensitive right now.'

Dr Caron looked at me, then glanced at her computer screen and responded thoughtfully, 'I don't think you can overreact to this. It looks like it could be pretty serious to me. Still, let's hope we can sort it out'.

I went cold—bone-shakingly, Lake Tahoe snow-fallingly cold. Holy shit, I thought. Surely we can't both have cancer? That would be bizarre. And then I recalled all the examples I knew of couples sharing their cancer journeys together. What makes us so special, I speculated, that we wouldn't both get struck down together?

Dr Caron went on to ask me a whole heap of personal questions about my sex life, past and present, and childbirth history. She then explained that that was why she doesn't let partners in at the onset. 'I need the truth,' she emphasised. Once the questions were over, she called her receptionist and asked her to send Philip in.

'Ok,' she stated to us both. 'What we have here is a potential problem. Looking at these scans, I have some serious concerns.' With that, she looked over at me. 'We need to go in and have a look, and we need to do it pretty quickly. I want to schedule an exploratory for next week and I'll need your permission to go forward with a complete hysterectomy should I find something sinister. If there is a problem in there, I want it out straight away, and while you are under a general we may as well get it done. So we're talking next Friday. Ok?'

'I'm not sure I have time next Friday, and I can't fit a hysterectomy in at the moment.' My voice sounded alien to me and it seemed to be coming from the other side of the room.

'This is more important than what is currently in your diary, Joan. What I'm seeing here is concerning me. I don't want you to panic, but I do think you should take it very seriously. If it's ovarian cancer, then we could be in trouble. Maybe changing your plans for next Friday would be a good idea.'

I became robotic. I left the surgery, confirmed the appointment with Dr Caron's receptionist and signed the initial paperwork. I remember getting instructions about turning up at the hospital.

A few days discomfort was mentioned, so I just cancelled my workload for the following Friday, but kept the five workshops booked in for the week after.

Philip and I arrived at the Wesley Hospital early on the Friday morning. It seemed strange to be the patient; it wasn't a role I was well-versed in at all. I was experienced at being in hospital waiting rooms but I was NEVER the patient. This all seemed out of place somehow. I went through the paperwork ritual without any emotion. I was as numb as numb could be. I handed over my jewellery to Philip and suggested he go and get something to eat. (I'd been fasting for hours and was ravenously hungry, but saw no point in both of us starving.) Our role reversal was complete as I watched him slip my wedding and eternity rings onto his little finger and head for the door. His shoulders were slumped and his head drooped low. He tugged at the door before he realised it opened outward, at which point he turned and threw me a wink and smile before shuffling out of sight towards the cafeteria.

Hospital processing is so repetitive. There were endless questions about my allergy to penicillin, and they repeatedly asked my name and date of birth. The anaesthetist arrived and asked all the same questions again. Who was I? When was I born? What happened if I was given penicillin? He was masked and gowned. I don't remember his name, but I'll never forget his gentle eyes and his genuinely caring voice. He was asking all the same questions, but the rote nature was missing. He seemed to really be interested.

He took my hand and looked gently down at me. 'Caron has explained the situation with your husband. This must be really tough. We'll look after you in there; try not to worry.' With that, he left.

An orderly wheeled me into the operating theatre. Dr Caron was looking very relaxed, sitting propped up against the wall wearing surgical scrubs and a cheery smile. She waved energetically at me as I was wheeled past her. I had already been given a pre-med and was feeling suitably relaxed. I made a supreme effort to return her smile but have no actual idea what my face was doing. It felt ok from the inside, though, a passable effort, I would hope. My new friend the anaesthetist was all set up and ready to go. Having been carefully transferred to the operating table, I looked up at him as he took my hand in his and started stroking the veins on the back of my hand. 'Start counting to ten for me, Joan,' said this now familiar, soft male voice, and before I got to three I was out.

I woke up some time later with the burning sore throat that is the first reminder that you've just had a surgical procedure. I felt woozy and disorientated and the female voice that I soon realised was coming from the nurse standing right next to my bed sounded like it was crossing great distance to get to me.

'Well hello there,' she said as she lifted my arm to start taking blood pressure readings. 'How are you feeling?'

'I've had better days,' I mumbled. Her hand felt cool as she moved my face sideways to enable access to my ear to take my temperature.

Her manner was compassionately brisk. I felt cared for, but was under no illusion as to the fact that her focus was on getting her job done.

The observations all complete, she attended to my request for some water, patiently holding the plastic cup and directing the straw to my mouth. My throat temporarily soothed, she patted my hand and turned to leave.

The vacated spot next to the bed was quickly filled by a set of the now familiar green surgical scrubs and I remember feeling a bit surprised, as Dr Caron had told me that there would be no results that day. The pathology would take a few days, so being a Friday, it would be the following week before we had any real information. 'Besides,' she'd explained. 'You'll be coming out of a general anaesthetic so you won't remember anything we talk about. It's better that I contact you next week when the pathology result are back and we can discuss everything in detail.'

Expecting to see Dr Caron anyway, I looked up to see a now very familiar set of eyes looking intently over the mask at me. I realised that I had never seen the face of the anaesthetist. He remains a 'masked hero' for me, even all these years later.

'How are you?' he enquired

'Guess we'll know in a few days,' I responded, trying to sound confident. My voice was crackly and shaky, and I'm not sure it was just because of the sore throat.

'I know Caron has said that she won't see you today,' he continued. 'That is her practice with all her patients. Please don't hold me to this, but I've worked with Caron on a number of these procedures and I just wanted to let you know that everything looked fine. We won't know for certain until the pathology comes back, of course, but with the situation with your husband

I thought you might have an easier weekend if I just gave you an update. Good luck with everything.'

My knight in green scrubs walked to the door and disappeared from my life.

I was indebted to him for his update and yes, we did have a reasonable weekend after that conversation. Well, we would have except the 'few days minor discomfort' predicted by Dr Caron turned out to be eight days or so of excruciating pain. I rested over the weekend, hoping that by Monday I would be feeling well again. Alas, it was to be the following Saturday before I could stand up without feeling like my insides were about to fall out and I could say goodbye to the incessant stomach cramps that came in painful waves—sometimes only minutes apart.

It was one of the longest weeks of workshops I have ever had.

The pathology results came in on the Wednesday and I knew instantly by the sound of Dr Caron's voice that everything was ok. Being well experienced in hearing difficult news, I felt my spirits rise when I heard those golden words, 'It's all good, everything was benign. Please take this the right way: I hope I never see you again. Good luck with Philip, and look after yourself.'

I put the phone back in my bag, clutched my stomach as another wave of cramps swept across my insides and breathed a sigh of relief. Drama over. As you were. Let's keep moving. And as if summoned, right on cue, the workshop group returned for the afternoon session.

Try to recognise the beloved stranger

Philip's treatment continued to hold the cancer, but the injection cycles were no less difficult. With each administration I hung on determinedly to the knowledge that the cancer was being slowed down. This was an important reminder that helped me manage those tumultuous two weeks following each injection.

It became evident that Philip's pain levels were heavily influenced by his emotional state. On his down days, his pain levels went up and on his good days, he managed with less pain medication. Any level of upset between us invariably had his pain hitting new highs. This realisation was very concerning.

Like all couples, we had our disagreements, but suddenly there was a new player in the ring. Pain. This knowledge was potentially very stifling for our relationship, as it quickly became apparent that any concept of 'air clearing' was no longer a viable option for us. Suddenly, it felt like I was constantly walking on eggshells as I avoided any subject that might escalate into even minor disagreement. While I realised on a rational level that this was out of Philip's control, on an emotional level it felt almost like subconscious blackmail.

In addition, the drugs appeared to be impacting quite markedly on Philip's rationality (previously one of his very strong points) which meant he was prone to making provocative statements and coming to unrealistic conclusions. The resulting fall out of this potent emotional cocktail had the potential to be catastrophic. Raising issues was too dangerous, but more and more issues kept raising their heads.

I tried a strategy of just 'copping it on the chin', reminding myself that the Philip I originally fell in love with was lost in the mire of cancer and drugs. All too often, that just resulted in a surge of resentment on my part (which in itself wasn't helpful) and there were situations that if not resolved had the potential to become very destructive. When a situation arose that clearly was impacting very negatively on our financial viability, I felt I had no choice but to raise it with him.

It had been our decision on moving in together that we could continue to maintain and operate our own bank accounts. However, with barely any work, Philip was not in a position to financially support himself. I had given him complete access to my bank accounts. This meant he could pay bills and draw money for expenses, hopefully without feeling 'kept'.

On checking the accounts myself, I found out that the balances were reducing rapidly. Also, I realised that he had been transferring money from an account allocated for tax payments and systematically draining it in order to pay for his flying lessons. Despite my trying to raise the issue delicately and sensitively, when it became evident what I was wanting to discuss, all hell broke loose.

I was subjected to a barrage of verbal abuse that I am convinced was aimed not so much at me in particular but to the women in his past. All the pus and slime of the financial losses that he believed had resulted from his marriage breakup suddenly erupted like a festering emotional boil and were splattered all over me. His fury at being 'ripped off', 'taken to the cleaners' and 'used' (as he angrily described his experiences) was unleashed. That, in his opinion, it was now his turn to get the handouts, was delivered in loud, clipped sentences. He again voiced his resentment about my financial success, snidely pointing out that I could easily just go and make more money, so what was I whingeing about?

This was not my Philip. I knew he had unresolved anger, but Philip was logical, rational, controlled and reasonable. I hated this stranger I was dealing with, but I still loved the man who was in there, fighting his own battle against hormone swings, uncertainty, and the whole out-of-controlness he was having to deal with.

Later that day I did one of the hardest things I've ever had to do in my life. I changed all the passwords on my accounts without mentioning a word to him. He never mentioned it either, though he had to know, and it must have been very difficult for him when next he went to get money from one of my accounts only to find that he no longer had access. Not wanting to leave him without funds to call his own (because no-one should be reduced to going 'cap in hand' to their partner) I started a practice of regularly transferring money to his account myself. Each time I transferred funds, my heart ached.

Illness takes so much—and so much of what it steals is invisible to the outside world.

Know that even superheroes need help

To say we were bouncing along is probably a fairly apt description. Nothing is ever all bad and, cancer aside, we had much in our lives to feel good about.

I was finding great solace in my work, and the contracts were flowing in from a variety of interesting areas. The workshop environment provided a helpful process of separation for me. My work gave me 'another life' to escape to.

My friend Helen, who had valiantly danced with two rounds of breast cancer, was enjoying a remission. My little farm was flourishing and, in my equestrian pursuits, I'd been promoted to the advanced show jumping class.

However, there was a limit to how much I could do and I suspect that, in a bid to keep one step ahead of the bills, I was constantly overstepping that limit. It was not uncommon for me to run five workshops a week and complete all the associated preparation work and accounts in the evenings and at the weekends. This was in addition to running the farm, managing the never ending demands of property maintenance and, as much as possible, going with Philip to medical appointments. It was evident to me that I was racing headlong towards burn out.

So we bounced through the day, we bounced through the weeks, and the months passed. Cancer was still our primary dance partner; however, we worked hard to try and function as best we could in other areas of our lives. The happy times were enjoyed and cherished, because to ignore them would have been foolhardy. The challenging times were faced with a constantly recycled sense of hope and optimism as we both strove to hang on to the courage and flexibility that the complex dance steps required.

Philip was finding much of the heavier farm work difficult and I had added skills like brush cutting and fence fixing to my repertoire. He was still able to engage with the animals, though, and was often the lead player in the evening feed regime. (Early mornings weren't easy for him, so I did the morning feeds alone.) He continued his one day per week in the local state politician's office. This helped to feed his voracious political appetite. It also provided him with a sense of purpose and the company of the good friends and like-minded people who were his co-workers in Geoff's office.

With the juggling of the business, the farm and some form of social/recreational interactions, time was scarce, especially when tests and/or hospital visits were added to the mix. I looked for ways to balance the workload, and one idea I clung to was to engage someone to help with housework. Of all the things that demanded my time, I felt that the most sensible thing to outsource was the housework. While I didn't dislike it, it wasn't a favourite activity, and I saw no point in outsourcing things as enjoyable as animal care and feeding or as lucrative as my consultancy work. To me, a cleaner to help in the house seemed not just obvious but necessary.

Sadly, Philip didn't share my view. Any mention of a cleaner either had him standing firm in his disapproval or descending into the black hole of inadequacy, declaring the excessive demands on my time to be his fault. This resulted in debilitating guilt (and therefore escalated pain levels as, as discussed, any degree of difficult emotion would instantly spark a pain reaction in him). Such painful results seemed counterproductive, so I constantly just dropped the subject and reached for the mop instead.

I couldn't understand his reluctance to have help in the house (and I still can't, although I do wonder if it was linked to his strong union background, which brought with it the belief that everyone should clean up after themselves). Even superheroes have helpers, and all I wanted was someone to come in once a week and clean the house. Our dogs, despite being working dogs, were welcome in the house, and left their furry appreciation all over the place. It was also a particularly dusty house and it only needed a couple of days for the furniture to be shrouded in a cover of dust thick enough to write a memoir in.

It was a discussion that was to be unsuccessfully revisited many times before I finally resolved it by just hiring somebody. When people ask me now about what things they might do to help themselves following a diagnosis, one of the first things I suggest is, if you can afford it, get help with the housework. Once the 'marvellous Marg' was installed, life changed so much for the better.

Marg found her way to us through an agency. During the interview with her, she revealed that her husband had died from cancer not quite twelve months earlier. I instantly stressed that she needed to make a decision around accepting the job based on her own needs.

'You don't need this job,' I emphasised, explaining where we were at with Philip's health.

'Maybe not,' she responded, 'but you need me. You will only get busier, and I know what you need in relation to cleaning and ensuring a 'safe' home for Philip infection-wise.'

Marg was much more than a cleaner. As Philip's illness progressed, she offered strong shoulders, loving arms and deeply understanding conversations.

Marg stayed with me until she met and fell in love with a new man. When they married, she moved away. Clearly the time was right for both of us and I was ready to take over the housework again.

Make everything an adventure

Our goal to go to India remained a strong focus for both of us. Philip had started to experience some difficult pain levels again and though the PSA results were still below the reading recorded when the cancer was diagnosed, they were on the rise. (I had come to learn that the severity of prostate cancer isn't so much gauged by the PSA level as it is by the fluctuation, so even though the numbers were relatively low, the rise was starting to become quite rapid, and that screamed danger.) We were both keen to go to the ashram and the '*vibhutti* prediction' experienced at Fresno felt like a message for both of us. Dr James was well on board, in fact highly encouraging, so together we made a plan, and Philip and I booked our tickets

We'd both travelled in India separately and I was excited about the prospect of going together. The thought of some time at Sai Baba's ashram was intriguing, and as we made the travel plans I got more and more excited. I had loved India when I first visited in 1997. I would go so far as to say it felt like a homecoming for me, and I was keen and ready to return to the land of my spirit.

We landed at New Delhi Airport full of anticipation—not so much for a 'cure' but for an adventure. The rise in the PSA levels coupled with Philip's increasing pain levels gave us clear messages that the cancer was learning some new and dangerous dance steps. We both felt that if we didn't go now, we might not manage the trip at all.

For me, India offers an invigorating rainbow assault on the senses. Nothing about your being is left untouched. As the plane taxied to the airport, I was reminded of my flight out some years before. I'd travelled aimlessly in India for some months and found the travel invigorating, exciting, confronting, extremely challenging and incredibly addictive. I remembered writing to a friend while relaxing in the British Airways plane en route for London (my next stop after New Delhi) and recounting some of my adventures. 'Leaving India,' I wrote, 'is like waking up from a really bad dream and realising you are safe at home in your own bed. And you know with every ounce of your being that you are going back again.' Here I was, back again. It felt wonderful.

India didn't disappoint me on this return visit. The first sense to awaken was the sense of smell as we exited the plane and were propelled by the bustling crowd into the airport terminal. Tingling nostrils happily picked up the array of aromas (both glorious and confronting) just slightly in advance of the reaction of the twitching eyes as they adjusted to the relentless activity of the colourful crowds. I scanned the sea of saris and kurta pyjamas, my eyes delighting in the bright colour of the women's silks, stark and vibrant against the white of the men's crisp, cotton outfits. My ears quickly tuned into the deafening human cacophony as the lilt of conversations blended into the crescendo of announcements and the bellowing of touts bidding for business. I breathed, I looked, I listened and I felt my spirit awaken.

I had booked us a hotel in New Delhi for the first few days of our stay, but had insisted on refusing the additional service of an airport to door car option. I wanted us to catch a local bus into the city centre and then make our way by foot (not a long distance) to the hotel. I wanted to immerse myself in India from the moment of my arrival. Somehow, an air-conditioned car felt too sterile. I remember literally skipping across the car park to find the bus to town. Philip followed a couple of paces behind me. I could sense that he shared my excitement. We both relished the thought of another adventure, and the activity of India was certain to supply us with that.

I danced up the steps of the bus and found myself face to face with a sea of smiling faces. By any western standard this bus was severely overloaded already, but I knew that by Indian standards there was still room for at least the same number of passengers again. As the only westerners on the bus, room was immediately found for us to sit down, and we occupied the newly vacated seats enthusiastically. (They were vacated by virtue of the previous occupier simply moving over and positioning themselves almost on the lap of the person next to them.) I was two rows behind Philip, both of us on the driver's side of the bus and we could easily maintain eye contact with each other as we were both, by necessity, sitting almost sideways on the seats.

The passengers kept coming and somehow just kept fitting in. The Indian population must be amazingly good at the hide and seek game 'sardines', as they just seem to be able to keep fitting people, animals and an array of household appliances into what is clearly an already full to the brim space.

Finally, it appeared that even the locals had decided that the bus was full. (Remember the roof space is also available, so all the windows were by now decorated with swinging feet as the 'penthouse passengers' settled in for the journey, dangling their legs over the side of the bus.) At this point, yet another group of would-be passengers approached the bus, lugging a large white object that revealed itself to be a washing machine. In true, 'everybody breathe in and this will fit' style, said washing machine was installed right in the doorway and the three men carrying it positioned themselves ready to catch it should the bus lurch violently (a situation almost guaranteed to happen). Finally, we were off.

I watched Philip as he engaged enthusiastically with the men around him. I realised that there were only three women on the bus and, having the additional visibility of also being a white woman, I found a multitude of eyes were fixed on me.

One of my memories of India is of being constantly stared at. I remembered during my previous visit, waking up on a train early one morning only to realise that my bunk was surrounded by men just staring. I instantly realised how Snow White must have felt, except she only had seven dwarfs watching her. I had at least twenty pairs of eyes. The Irish woman I was travelling with at the time commented when she woke to the same audience, 'It'll be strange going home and not being stared at, won't it? We'll start to feel dead ordinary again.'

I never found the staring intimidating. It appeared to me to be a case of harmless curiosity, and as I settled back into the fraction of the seat that I'd been allocated, I prepared myself for 'India as a couple', which I anticipated would be a very different experience to India alone. My anticipation was very quickly confirmed.

While Philip chatted, I kept a fairly low profile. Culturally, it is expected that the man will do the communicating and, in complete contrast to my personality, I accepted the reality of this and busied myself in two of my favourite pastimes, observing and daydreaming. Watching the world outside the feet-bordered window was fascinating and I completely failed to contain my excitement when a brightly-decorated elephant, complete with rider, emerged from a side street. I leapt up from my seat, waving my arms and pointing with great vigour at this incredible sight. My fellow passengers, clearly curious about what could have set the white woman off, all glanced in the direction of my energetic pointing, only to sigh knowingly and then return to their previous activities. I guess an elephant in India isn't a big deal, but to me it was enormous (both literally and symbolically). The elephant is one of my favourite animals, and I marvelled that one had appeared so soon into our visit to welcome us (and had dressed for the occasion).

Frustratingly, nothing else outside the window looked in the least bit familiar and it soon became apparent to me that my memory had deceived me, or that New Delhi had changed enormously, or we'd caught the wrong bus, because I had no idea where we were or where we might be going.

I alerted Philip to the fact that we might in fact already be lost (an amazing achievement given that we'd only been in the country for 45 minutes) and he immediately started engaging the assistance of fellow passengers. He used that blend of stilted English, (dropping any superfluous words) that travellers adopt when they are in countries where people don't speak their language and they have no idea of the native tongue. It was amusing to listen to this highly educated, extremely erudite man saying slowly and clearly things like 'we go to here', carefully demonstrating 'here' on a map. 'You help us?'

Clearly, all our fellow passengers had recently signed some sort of traveller assistance treaty, because we were immediately mobbed by an array of would-be helpers, all with different advice. Pens were produced and our map was customarily scribbled all over, streets and landmarks rapidly disappearing beneath arrows and carefully drawn Hindi symbols. Within minutes, the map was rendered useless but the dedicated assistance continued energetically, questions and instructions being constantly relayed to the driver in enthusiastic tones.

Without warning, the bus stopped. Fortunately, the washing machine minders had remained focused on their task and the appliance survived to complete another cycle. Gentle helping hands ushered us down the driver's side of the aisle while our backpacks were passed from person to person at head height, like some aerial game of tunnel ball. We were carefully deposited on the side of the dirt road. As the bus left, an enormous cloud of dust enveloped us. The crowd that just seconds ago had been our travel companions waved frantically, calling what I can only imagine to be fond farewells and good wishes. Silence descended. We stood facing each other, no idea where we were, our map (carefully returned to us) of absolutely no use, and we both burst out laughing.

'Welcome to India,' I giggled.

'At which point do I get to enquire why we didn't organise the car to pick us up at the airport?' returned Philip laughingly, clearly feeling good humoured and unfazed by our experiences so far.

Our laughter was suddenly punctuated by a cry familiar to both of us. 'Rickshaw? Rickshaw?' called a voice, and there, emerging from the dust, was the delightfully ubiquitous 'carriage and cycle' that for me is as synonymous with India as a good curry and the amazing painted elephant. Yep, I'd come home!

New Delhi, it seemed, was in the grip of progress, and the construction of an underground train network had temporarily closed the bus terminal in the centre of the city. Consequently, we'd been deposited (none too shabbily) on the city outskirts. Sadly, we had no idea whether we were north, south, east or west and, with our map transformed into a primary school class drawing project, we were at a loss as to how to explain where we were going.

Negotiating a fare with a rickshaw driver is always interesting. Our humanitarian need to abide by a 'fair work/fair pay' guideline became somewhat challenged when we had no idea where we were or where our destination was. We didn't feel in much of a position to assess 'fair' anything, and as patient as our chariot driver was, the language barrier was making for some very interesting negotiations. I was somewhat sceptical that our driver had actually understood which hotel we were referring to. Nor was I convinced by his claims that the hotel had burnt down the day before and he would therefore need to take us to another one.

It was some hours later that we finally arrived at the hotel I'd booked, and of course it hadn't burnt down at all. We were delayed by a number of conversations with a variety of rickshaw drivers (all holding firm to the fire tragedy) and a lengthy sojourn in a tour office (where we were eventually dropped off and abandoned by the rickshaw wallahs).

The tour office was clean and comfortable, but it wasn't the hotel I'd booked and paid for, so I was not as keen to spend time there as the tour guide wished. Seeing the advantage of a captive audience, he quickly produced brochures and outlined an array of 'very cheap and reasonable' fees. We both tried, unsuccessfully to sway the committed sales man away from his task.

'We would just like to go to our hotel,' pleaded Philip. 'We don't want to book a tour.'

Philip and I were not tour people. Our travel preference is to go our own way, in our own time, at our own pace. In recognition of the cultural requirement for the men to do all the business, I initially stayed out of the conversation, but as Philip's repeated pleas fell on deaf ears, I felt compelled to try to help.

'We're happy to consider a tour tomorrow, after we've had some rest.' I needed to make no effort to sound tired. The long journey from Brisbane had caught with me. 'But for now, could you please help us get to our hotel?' For emphasis, I laid my head on my arms and sighed.

'Certainly, madam,' came the polite reply. 'But first, please look at this tour; it is very good, I assure you.'

Our frustration that we had finally found someone who spoke perfect English but whose focus was on something completely unrelated to what we were wanting was escalating. And then he lit up a cigarette.

'I have cancer. Please put that out.' Philip's voice was terse.

The cigarette was immediately extinguished. Not so the sales man's determination.

Finally, he won. We signed up for a tour of the old city for the following day and handed over the money. *Voila*, a car appeared, instructions were given to the driver and we were transported to our hotel. It was that easy. Maybe we should have tried that two hours previously.

By this time, our amusement at our predicament had degenerated into pure frustration. Philip was looking exhausted and I was fed up. We weren't happy campers, and I was wondering what stupid planet of optimism I'd been on when I had refused the car from the airport. However, despite our frustration and exhaustion, the irony of arriving at the hotel in an air-conditioned car, the very event I had been so keen to avoid, was not lost on us.

We checked into the hotel to raised eyebrows from the guy at the desk who had the hide to ask what had taken us so long when our plane had arrived on time (he knew that because he had checked). We retreated rapidly to our room. I exhaustedly threw myself face-down on the bed, only to be immediately reminded of yet another fact about India—the beds are rock hard, and I mean rock hard.

I almost knocked myself out.

Find peace where you can—and
don't question it too much

Despite all the frustrations around our arrival, we quickly settled into the Indian pace of life, which oscillates from frenetic (in terms of the traffic) to totally chilled (in terms of people's responses to anything). I found myself enjoying both.

We made our way to Puttaparthi via a combination of local buses and local trains. It was not luxurious travel by any stretch of the imagination, and despite Philip's insistence that he wanted to travel that way, it became quickly evident that his pain levels weren't going to make continuing on a 'grass roots' trip possible. On arrival at the village of the ashram, we decided that we would continue our travels, as much as possible, by private car. This was still not the most comfortable option in India as the roads are rough and full of potholes, but at least it gave us options to have stops and rest breaks, a requirement that the public transport system couldn't accommodate.

Puttaparthi is a village built around the ashram. It has the appearance of a chilled-out market town. Colourful stalls line the streets and the patrons, hailing from all over the world, wander slowly and purposefully through the array of wares and food stalls. Nothing is rushed; everything is laid back. I loved the atmosphere. I loved seeing the array of cultures, religions (one day delighting in seeing a Catholic priest, a Muslim, a Hindu and a Buddhist all laughingly conversing) and lifestyles all interacting. There appeared to be no barriers of beliefs here at all. Every day, I felt I was living in a heartening version of Blue Mink's musical melting pot.

Philip was experiencing significant discomfort, and his sleep patterns just wouldn't right themselves. Whether it was prolonged jet lag or whether it was a symptom of the cancer we didn't know. It was probably a combination of the two. We decided that staying in communal accommodation at the ashram was probably going to be too much for him, so we opted instead for a hotel in the village and made daily pilgrimages to partake of the ashram events.

We had been lucky in that Sai Baba was in attendance for our stay. Our day became a steady and soothing ritual of attending morning Bhajans (chants), returning to the hotel for Philip to rest and then going back to the ashram in the afternoon/evening. The ashram separates men and women, each gender having their own entrance and gathering points. It is also requested that for the time you are within the ashram itself, all visitors dress in traditional Indian attire.

Knowing that I'm not elegant enough to carry off a sari, I opted for the loose pants and extended tunic combination that is known as a *salwar kameez* and enjoyed my forays into the marketplace to procure outfits which I wore throughout my time in India. Philip cut a dashing figure in the crisp white kurta pajamas worn by the men. It was a fascinating visual contrast at the ashram. One side of the gathering was brilliantly colourful and vibrant as the women's silks mixed and merged with each other, while the men's side shone in the stark white sea of freshly laundered white cotton. Philip was impossible to find in the crowd. A dark haired man with a dark moustache clad all in white, he was one of several hundred, and they all looked the same.

Not so to Sai Baba it turned out, as Philip returned to our hotel room one morning looking happily excited. 'He looked at me!' he exclaimed, his face beaming.

Of course I knew who 'he' was. Philip was adamant that during the Bhajans, his eyes had met Sai Baba's. 'He knows I'm here,' continued Philip.

I have to say that any attempts I'd made to attract Sai Baba's attention had failed, but maybe Philip was right. In any event, he rode on the high of the encounter for hours.

We both fell into the rhythm of this life with ease. Philip's rest periods could be quite lengthy and I would amuse myself sipping tea on the balcony of our room, watching life go by on the street below. I noticed that the rickshaws were all numbered, and I set myself a project to spot them in sequential order starting with number one and seeing how high I could go. Over the eight days of our visit I successfully clocked one to one hundred and eighty nine. I became deeply entrenched in this project, and even now recall my excitement when the next number in my sequential search ambled past my vantage point.

My life had been incredibly busy for years. As a single parent, a full time employee and a part time student (both my under graduate and post graduate degrees had been gained through part time study while working full time and raising my girls) and more recently a self-employed/part time farmer/part time carer, time to 'sit and be' had never been available in abundance. I surprised myself by how quickly I adjusted to this very different and rather enjoyable pace of life.

On the afternoons when he felt well enough, Philip would have massages and treatments at the local Ayurvedic (an ancient Indian form of medicine) centre. He responded well to these visits and seemed to enjoy some respite from his discomfort for some hours after visiting.

We had decided that we would arrive in Puttaparthi without any plans and just see what unfolded. Other than a timeframe for returning home, we had no other commitments or limitations, and if we spent the whole six weeks at the ashram that would be fine. If we left earlier, then we would just embark on some travel. It all depended on how Philip felt and what we decided we wanted to do.

Our eighth day had commenced like all others since our arrival. We spent time at the ashram and then wandered back to the hotel room. The marketplace was buzzing and the sounds, sights and smells were soothing as we chatted. Neither of us made mention of any thoughts of leaving. We were both enjoying the ashram experience and being in Puttaparthi in general.

That night we both had identical dreams. In them, Sai Baba called us to him and said it was time for us to go. He was kind, yet emphatic. When we compared notes the next morning, we were both stunned by the total duplication of the dreams.

We were discussing the dreams over breakfast when we were joined at the table by a German man.

'It's time for you to go.' He started the conversation by getting straight to the point. 'Sai Baba has said.'

He went on to explain that he had visited the ashram numerous times, each time knowing that the timeframe for his visit would be determined by Sai Baba, and each time it was. 'He comes in our dreams and tells us when our time here is over,' he continued. 'It's normal. Safe travels to you'.

Having imparted that news, he made his way to a vacant table over by the window and ordered his meal.

We finished our breakfast, and without any further hesitation, organised a car, checked out of the hotel and headed off for Bangalore.

It's a long drive, and the driver stopped en route for a bathroom break and to allow us to stock up on cool drinks. Before setting off again, our taxi driver leaned over between the two front seats to face Philip. 'I have present for you, from Sai Baba,' he said.

'For me!' exclaimed Philip, intrigued.

'Yes,' replied our driver and handed over two small packages. 'It is some more *vibhutti*,' he said. 'Sai Baba is sorry he couldn't see you himself, and as he is concerned that you are running out, he asked me to give you this from him.'

Philip and I were in shock. Had the driver just presented the *vibhutti*, we would have dismissed it as some marketing ploy, but he seemed to know that Philip had been using the magic ash and, more interestingly, seemed to be aware that his supplies were running short. Philip had used the *vibhutti* that Gretchen had given him every day, and until we arrived in India the original amount hadn't decreased at all. He mentioned to me once, 'This stuff keeps reproducing', and according to the accounts of many people, in fact, it does. However, on arrival in India it had gone down rapidly until replenished that day in the taxi.

Do what you love for as long as possible

Our travels in India were both glorious and difficult. Philip's pain levels were increasing, particularly after any travel on the bumpy Indian roads. I could see that he frequently struggled to get through the day when we first arrived at places. Transport was a nightmare, and we punctuated road trips with extended rest stays to assist him to re-group and try to relax his now complaining body.

I suggested on a few occasions that we abandon any more travel and just see out our time in India in one spot, or even consider cutting the trip short and heading home.

Philip's refusal of either suggestion was determined. 'It's becoming pretty apparent that I may never get back to this country,' he lamented philosophically one day. 'And I think we should do our best to visit the places that are important to us.'

During the period of our stay, Australia was playing India at cricket (in Australia) and, an avid fan of the game, Philip would make updating himself with scores a priority every morning. His daily stroll through the marketplace of any village we were in would quickly turn into a general update as locals realised that the dark haired Australian in the kurta pyjamas had access to the latest scores.

'What's the score, Philip?' would ring out across the marketplace, and Philip, keen to engage in a conversation about one of his passions, would immediately respond with the latest information. This invariably continued to a full-blown conversation and I was touched by the total absence of any competitiveness. If Australia had done well overnight, the Indian market stall owners would rejoice loudly, and if India had given the Aussies a run for their money Philip's face would be beaming as he celebrated, arm in arm, with local fans. It was a wonderful demonstration of collaboration, and I was heartened by such enthusiastic displays of appreciation for game skills rather than team scores.

Cricket discussions always ended in tea and I would frequently find Philip tucked away behind a curtain somewhere sipping, laughing and chatting. Despite sometimes having experienced an almost total lack of sleep the night before, Philip's face glowed during these interactions. In those moments, any thoughts I had of rushing home early drifted away on the wafts of smoke emanating lazily from the handmade beakers that held the piping hot beverage.

But for the pain of the Philip's cancer, it was an idyllic time. We had no timeframes, nowhere we needed to be for some time yet, and no travel plans. We moved on as the urge took us, our only notion being to try to get as far south as Kerala. We both had a desire to visit the backwaters and the lure of a houseboat for a few days was incredibly appealing to us.

I have vivid recollections of filling the passing time by occupying myself in deliciously senseless ways. One day, I sat mesmerised for hours and hours, watching through the window of our hotel as the ironing wallah across the road went about his daily duties.

Each time the ironing pile would reach a manageable proportion, along would come several more baskets of clothes in need of his attention. It seemed like endless, thankless work, yet not even a hint of frustration was ever emitted by the dedicated man with the iron in this hand. He maintained an almost hypnotic rhythm and the cloth under his hands responded by abandoning its creases in favour of a crisp, smooth look.

Periodically, the patient ironing wallah would carefully and mindfully replace the cooling coals in the hollow iron with new red hot nuggets and then the rhythmic movements would begin again. The finished products were perfect, with not a hint of a crease to be seen and the hanging rack on his right hand side would be continually filled and then just as diligently emptied. It was a collective effort. There was someone to deliver the washing, someone to iron the clothes, someone to take the ironed clothes and deliver them to their owner so the whole, endless cycle could no doubt begin again. I sat in a high backed chair in the window facing the scene, watching as avidly as I might watch a favourite movie. Who could ever have guessed that ironing could be such a spectator sport?

One afternoon in Bangalore, Philip and I wandered the streets of the village. Our nostrils delighted in the aromas of the hand-rolled incense and we strolled from stall to stall watching with interest the women immersed in their task. Again, the process seemed endless, always more incense to roll, the pile of completed sticks regularly being collected as new materials for more production were delivered.

I marvelled in the patience of these people. There was no rush or hurry and I wondered if I would be able to continue this relaxed existence when I returned to the frenetic world of work waiting for me back in Australia.

A young voice slipped gently into my awareness. 'Do you want to see a koala?' he enquired. I looked down to see a cherub-faced boy who I guessed to be about six years old. His skin was grubby, his hair matted and his clothes several sizes too small, except for his boots—he was swimming in those.

'A koala?' I questioned disbelievingly.

'Yes, a koala.' His voice had taken on a degree of firmness and he repeated his announcement with more emphasis.

'But there aren't any koalas in Bangalore,' I noted teasingly.

'Yes,' he implored. 'There are. I'll show you'.

Philip and I followed the child through the back streets. We both knew there would be no koala, but we were intrigued to find out what he wanted to show us. We kept an eye out for reference points, knowing we'd have to find our way back, and we stayed within well populated areas. It all felt very safe. We knew we were being conned; we just didn't know what we would be expected to buy at the end of it.

Our koala chase concluded at an incense stall run by the young boy's family. He introduced us to his parents and his sisters and he proudly showed us the impressive range of incense on display. 'So,' I enquired jokingly. 'Where's the koala, then?'

Our young friend giggled. 'In the zoo, madam,' he responded and took off down the street at a half running, half ambling pace.

We brought incense from his family's stall and then followed our tracks back to the hotel.

As rest stops allowed Philip to recuperate, we'd set about tackling the next leg of the adventure. We kept heading south, finally reaching Kerala, a place we'd both wanted to visit for some time. It didn't disappoint.

'Ah, Kipling country,' sighed Philip as we alighted from the boat that had carried us to Cochin. 'All my life I've wanted to spend time in Kipling country.'

The days drifted by. We were both delighted that we'd made it to the glorious southern tip and, having now spent some weeks in India, we had successfully made the 'energy adjustment' and were happy to amble instead of rush. We'd sit for hours and watch and wonder, and we seemed to have been completely cured of any need to be entertained.

Sunsets were spent watching the fishermen cast their nets, mornings were languished away in beachside cafes, and the time in between just passed in glorious no-rush nothingness. With our travels over for a while, Philip relaxed and his pain levels noticeably subsided. I frequented the local book shop and read avidly (when I wasn't watching something aimlessly). As time moved on, we remembered our desire to cruise the backwaters and our hotel owner who (like all Indian hotel owners) doubled as a tour guide, leapt to the task as soon as we mentioned it to him.

Our first sighting of the rattan house boats brought an enormous smile to my face. They were character personified. With massive awnings, inviting day beds and a cosy, comfortable cabin, the whole thing screamed 'more relaxation!' and I couldn't wait to step aboard.

Philip and I were the only guests and we had a staff of four to look after us. In theory, we could sit back and be waited on hand and foot, but such a situation has never been my style and, of course, union official Philip was having no part to play in 'servitude and slavery'. The boat crew rebelled at first, protesting when we attempted to do anything for ourselves, but quickly realised that we weren't trying to take their jobs, just merely engage with them and be part of the team. At that point, they welcomed us warmly.

With six of us to run the boat, there was plenty of time for us all to relax, and Philip spent hours sleeping on the bow while I, well stocked with books from the merchant in Cochin, idled my time away turning pages. In the afternoons I would partake of cooking lessons from our 'singing chef' (he was forever singing or whistling) and as the days passed, we produced gourmet feasts that progressively got ever more complex and delicious as our communication and my cooking skills developed.

Philip was delightfully engaged in sharing language skills of his own and was heavy into Hindi lessons which he was swapping for guidance with English. We floated through rice paddies, stopping at tiny villages where we would be greeted by squeals of delight from the local children. We played games with the kids and traded trinkets with the adults, and most of all we shared life. This was life in the backwaters. We were accepted by the locals, our crew acted as guides and interpreters and we relished the opportunity to engage, not just observe.

Philip and I would have made terrible tourists. We were travellers; we always had been. Travelling requires risks and it demands that you trust. I've returned from my travels with stories that have made friends cringe, and on reflection I can see how dangerous or irresponsible some of my behaviours might appear to the listener. That said, they have led me to adventures, to meeting amazing people, to sharing lifestyles and stories, and my life has been inexplicably enriched because of them.

Philip was a travelling soul mate. We were both mindful, but we weren't afraid to step into the abyss that transcended culture and supplied endless gifts of amazing experiences. We both held experiences in much higher esteem than possessions, and our houseboat time was enriching, enlightening and revitalising in terms of the people, interactions and activities that it afforded us.

We were both disappointed when we found ourselves drifting back into the harbour and realised our time here was finished. It was a teary goodbye to our crew. We'd shared our time as equals, and we parted as friends. They had taught us and looked after us and we had done the same for them.

We caught a train back to Mumbai and from there boarded our flight home. We had gone to India in search of solace. We hoped that our experience with Sai Baba would give us hope. We wanted to light up our souls with adventure and we wanted to remind ourselves that it's who we are, not what we have that makes us real and authentic. India didn't let us down. She gave us all that in spades, and we returned ready to take the floor, listen to the music and step into the next level of the dance.

Returning home always presents its own form of culture shock, and the sudden transportation from the colour, activity, pace and disorganisation of India to the relative calm and control of Brisbane shook our brain neurons a bit.

We had an appointment with Dr James and Philip needed to get a PSA test, which he organised a few days after we arrived home. A week after landing in Brisbane, we were back at the Wesley Hospital for our appointment. The PSA was continuing to rise. The pain levels had pretty much indicated that the cancer was on the move again and Dr James suggested the commencement of some radiation therapy. It was duly organised to start the following week.

We were both in a bit of shock. It wasn't so much that we'd expected a miraculous cure in India—Philip's pain throughout the trip was a clear indication that this wasn't happening. It just felt like a rather violent thrust back to reality to be faced with treatment requirements immediately upon our return.

A few days later, we arrived at the radiation ward for the start of his radiotherapy. Our ship had circumnavigated a whole new land of difficulty and come back to cancer. I was heartily sick of this rotten cruise.

And then the next storm blew in.

Remember that you're not the only ones on this journey

'It's back,' said the voice over the phone.

I didn't have to ask what or back where. Helen's voice was very familiar to me and 'it' was a demon we both knew all too well.

Helen's cancer had originally been diagnosed some years and two remissions ago. For this third assault, we both knew that the cards weren't looking in her favour.

I'd gotten to know her oncologist quite well over the years and it felt distressingly familiar to be walking back into his consulting rooms. I scanned the family photos again—the same faces and poses. His wife and children hadn't aged at all, yet it seemed like the rest of us had all lived several lifetimes.

Helen's scans weren't good, and the cancer was extensive and aggressive. It was decided to fight fire with fire and be equally aggressive in our medical response. I could feel Helen's fear.

The chemo ward was also a disturbingly familiar place. The ritual of packet opening and sterile cloth positioning sparked horrifying memories and Helen's attempts at bravery and humour were admirable but often hollow. We'd done this trip twice before, and the third time was three times too many.

I had a knitting project on the go, which I would often take with me to the chemo ward as the hours spent sitting with Helen provided a good opportunity to ensure the deadline for the shawl I was creating would be met. Helen watched the progress with great interest. Herself an accomplished knitter, she recognised the complexity of the pattern I was following, and was encouraging of my progress. The finished item was almost the size of a double bed, so as the project continued it got more and more difficult to transport and unpack safely (as in avoiding spillages and staining of the gleaming white flowing piece). I knitted like my life depended on it, only taking time out to procure us a 'real' coffee (we both refused to drink the instant stuff off the trolley) from the coffee shop.

On one chemo visit, I advised Helen that I would be working in North Queensland for the next scheduled date but that she wasn't to worry as Philip would pick her up from home and come with her to treatment. (I hadn't been very much in favour of this, but he insisted and wouldn't accept any of my arguments that his attending chemo might be a little too confronting.)

'Does he knit too?' Helen enquired.

I laughed. 'Of course he doesn't,' I replied.

'Thank God for that,' she stated firmly. 'It's like being at a public beheading. I'll enjoy the break from the knitting needles.'

Round three of Helen's dance with this disease was a horror experience of such magnitude that it made rounds one and two look like the warm up sessions (and rounds one and two had been pretty horrendous). It was a lethal mix that was brought in to face off with the cancer and the treatment was hard on Helen.

I remembered reading a comment by an oncologist that the best they hope for is that at the end of the treatment, the cancer is dead and the patient is only half dead. I could see Helen going downhill, not just from the treatment, but from the sum total of nine years of her life having been dictated to by this monster. She had had enough. That much was evident to all of us.

A single mum with two beautiful girls, Helen's primary focus was her daughters and staying alive and becoming well so she could enjoy being part of their lives. So, with the driving force of a determined mother, Helen pursued health with everything she had.

The oncologist was examining the latest scans. I could see he was troubled. I could also see he was tired. We had an evening appointment, as Helen remained determined to continue going to work. His surgery hours seemed endless and I started to think he might have perfected the art of cloning, as it wasn't unusual to have him pop into the ward late at night during periods of Helen's hospitalisation. I couldn't imagine how one man managed to work such hours and be in so many places.

He raised his glance from the scan reports and looked at me. 'Can't you talk her into giving up work?' he pleaded.

I looked at Helen. We were both crying. 'No,' I whispered.

Helen and I had talked briefly about her giving up work. She had raised the subject during the previous chemo treatment. 'I think the doc thinks I should be taking up my sick leave.' She'd thrown the comment randomly into a completely unrelated conversation.

'Why don't you?' I enquired.

'The day I can't get up and go to the work is the day I'll die.' Her tone was pure terror. 'While I'm going to work, there is a chance I can convince myself that I'll make it. It's keeping me going.'

I dropped the subject. I think I understood what she was saying, and even if I didn't, I could hear how important it was to her to have the driving force of employment to sustain her energetically.

However, there was no doubt that her health was going backwards. I knew that the chemo was largely responsible for that. This new mix was more brutal than anything she'd had before. I went into practical mode and started cooking meals for the family. Helen was always honest and entertaining with her feedback. 'Loved the lamb pie,' she exclaimed one day. 'I even managed to keep that down, enjoyed eating it and hung onto it. We'd love more of that, please.'

I happily complied and got cooking. Despite my vegetarianism, I knew that the family enjoyed meat and, from my perspective, it was about getting food into them all.

'How do you taste it to make sure it's ok before you give it to us?' asked Helen in the same conversation, 'I don't. Philip does,' I answered.

'Oh the boy's back on the meat then, is he?' she laughed.

When I'd announced that Philip and I were both going to be vegan, Helen had almost fallen off the chair in surprise. 'He won't last,' she declared. 'He's a meat man if ever I met one.'

She was right. Philip had gradually brought meat back into his diet, and after allowing myself to experience much angst over it, I had decided to let it be. I still questioned the wisdom of red meat in his health situation and continued to be happily vegetarian myself, but I cooked the much sought-after lamb pie for Helen and the girls, and naturally there was always an extra one for Philip. I soothed my own concerns by ensuring all ingredients were organic. They all seemed happy.

I did feel some variety was called for though, so one meal that I lovingly delivered to Helen was a vegetable cobbler. 'Ummmm, the girls were intrigued by last night's dinner,' Helen mused when I arrived to pick her up the following day for her chemo visit. 'They ate it, but wondered if perhaps you were just trying to save time by adding the dessert to the main meal?' She slid the empty dish across the kitchen bench at me. 'They were still giggling about it this morning. They think you may have lost your marbles.'

Don't expect to be invincible

Life felt like one big hospital visit. Philip had changed oncologists and was into his second round of radiation. The first round provided some short term relief, but the bone tumours were slowly spreading. Dr James assured us that the hormone treatment was still worth continuing as the evidence was suggesting that it was slowing things down, but the monster had woken up. Though it was still sluggish, it was highly likely that the next wave of force was imminent. Dr James decided it was time for Philip to go to the next level of oncology, and we were referred to Dr Maree.

Dr Maree was to be the one to walk side by side with us to the conclusion of this journey and, even now as I reflect on our interactions with her, I know we couldn't have had a better tour guide.

Picking doctors is an individual thing, and Philip and I were quite opposite in what we sought. Philip wanted direct and honest, no frills, tell it like it is and get it over with, whereas I needed gentleness, understanding, a sense of connection and caring. Dr Maree was the perfect package, because she quickly assessed us and interacted with us in ways that were consistent with our individual needs.

She never hid the tough news from Philip and would talk frankly and honestly with him. She never delivered even one tiny fragment of difficult news to me without holding my hand. She had summed up who we were and she became the doctor we both needed.

She made two suggestions at our first consultation. The first one was that Philip had another round of radiation (she referred him to the Royal Brisbane Hospital for that) and the second one was that he started a regular bone density treatment. The cancer was compromising his bone strength and the radiation had the potential to impact on that even more, so introducing a drug to help hold the bone density seemed logical. She made some phone calls and directed us to go immediately to the hospital next door for the first administration.

Directions in hand, we made our way through the covered breezeway that connected the two hospitals and took the lift to the appointed floor. Exiting into a maze of corridors, we followed signs to the room number we were seeking and turned innocently through a doorway, only to emerge in hell.

I couldn't breathe; it felt like my chest had collapsed and I could feel myself sweating. I grabbed Philip's arm. 'I have to sit down.' My words were barely audible even to me. My blood pressure had instantly dropped and my head was spinning. I could see people looking at me and a nurse had started to make her way over to us. I was shaking uncontrollably as the nurse guided me to a chair. Not just A chair but one of THE chairs. I wanted to run, I tried to get up, but my legs wouldn't hold me. I was vaguely aware of slight pressure on my shoulders. I was being gently held in the chair and a soft female voice was whispering, 'It's OK. We'll look after you'.

I wanted to scream, but I didn't have the energy. I didn't need looking after; I needed to get out of here. Philip was standing in front of me and I could see from his facial expression that he understood what was happening for me.

'She just needs a minute.' He knelt down beside the chair on the opposite side to the nurse. 'I'm the patient, this is my wife. We're sorry; we didn't realise that the treatment would be administered in the chemo ward. This has been quite a shock for her.'

Two fucking days in a row! Two people I loved dearly! I'd worked hard to be strong and stoic throughout all the treatments because, as I kept reminding myself, I wasn't the patient and I was going to walk away from this. The chemo ward had different ideas that day. It smashed my stoicism to smithereens and threw it straight back into my shocked face. 'Strong, are you?' it screamed at me. 'Well, take that!' I felt like I'd been physically hit. Somebody got me a cup of tea, and as the seconds built to minutes, my heartbeat gradually slowed down and my capacity to breathe returned. I stretched back in the recliner rocker that was meant for a patient and closed my eyes.

'OK, you bastard,' I resolved, seeing cancer as an ugly, deformed gremlin in my mind's eye. 'Next round, here we come.' I closed my eyes and worked hard to just get my shit back together.

I was aware that everybody in the room was watching me, not with curiosity, but with care and compassion. Nobody judged. I knew I'd just had a public meltdown and it was alright because everybody knew that next time it could be them. With time, I vacated the 'treatment chair', took the visitor's chair beside it and resigned myself to watch with sadness as the familiar ritual of packet opening and sterile cloth laying was undertaken.

Helen's chemo had been the day before. Philip's bone density treatment was a monthly administration, and his radiation wasn't scheduled to start until the following week. All things going well, I had six whole hospital-free days coming up. I worked hard to hold on to the positive side of that.

*Make a choice as to what impact you are
going to have on the people around you*

We were back in the nuclear medicine ward for more scans. This time, my intention was to stay with Philip all day, and my phone helpfully decided to stay in one piece.

We arrived early and settled ourselves in for a rather long day of waiting, tests, waiting, results, waiting, oh and did I mention waiting? The usual array of out of date magazines was on hand, and despite the early hour of the day, the waiting room was full.

Everybody was in pairs—a patient and a support person. All those undergoing the scans would need a lift home. The pairs cocooned themselves in their individual pods of pain and confusion. The very fact that they were here in the nuclear medicine ward was evidence enough that things were not good on the health front. These weren't 'routine' tests; these were 'we already know there is a problem and we're establishing just how bad it is' tests.

There was no interaction other than the occasional sympathetic connection of eyes as new couples arrived (and for many, even that level of interaction was too difficult, so they remained distant by keeping their eyes down). Nobody spoke. I guess we had all decided there wasn't anything to say. 'How are you?' was too scary, and 'nice day isn't it?' felt ridiculous. Nobody in the nuclear medicine ward was expecting to have a 'nice day' that day. I flipped through a magazine mindlessly.

The book in my bag languished as I had so far been unable to muster the energy to open my bag. Philip gazed off into space, our only connection being the occasional brushing of hands as he reached out to check that I hadn't somehow disappeared. Wherever possible, every waiting pair had left at least one chair's space between them and the nearest other waiting pair. We all felt too overwhelmingly connected by our medical plight; we weren't seeking a tangible connection with each other at all.

The room felt heavy and suffocating. The array of hospital smells launched successive attacks on our nostrils. Just in case anybody had somehow found the fortitude to actually forget where they were, the next sweep of disinfectant cruised past, bringing us instantly back to the discomfort of the room. It was 8.00 am on a weekday morning, and while everybody had somewhere else they'd rather be, we all knew we are stuck here, together, until well into the afternoon.

The glass sliding doors silently slid open and those of us still retaining any level of curiosity glanced up to observe the newcomers as they entered the room. She strode in confidently. The hem of her floral cotton dress swirled around her calves and her wide-brimmed straw hat sat playfully askew on her head. Her face was beaming. Her smile so totally contagious that people instantly moved beyond their practised glance of anonymity and, unable to control their attraction to her, allowed the corners of their mouths to curl upwards in a returning greeting smile.

Her companion followed close behind. He was bent over, his gaze perpetually downwards so he had no option but to examine the polished tiles on the floor. He shuffled slowly, and his oversized jacket hung loosely over baggy trousers. He looked dishevelled and worn out as he obediently followed the rose print floral dress. The woman found two seats and took some time to settle him into one of them. They appeared to be somewhere in their late 60s or early 70s, and I estimated that they were the oldest people in the room by some years.

Having settled her partner comfortably, the floral woman proceeded to circumnavigate the room, greeting people personally and offering to get cups of water, or to bring over a different array of magazines. I watched intently. With my communication consultant hat firmly in place, I was fascinated to notice the connection she was making. Cocoons burst open as individuals interacted with her, accepting her offer of water or reading material, responding to her questions energetically and engaging in small talk.

Ah,' I decided. 'They are volunteers, here to help brighten up our day.' I was impressed by the woman's warmth and genuine caring, and I assumed her male companion was just having some difficulty getting started this morning.

Within minutes, the atmosphere in the room had changed. People were now chatting to each other, and the vacant chairs between couples had disappeared as bottoms slid across so as to better allow their owners to converse with their neighbour. In a matter of a very short space of time, the woman in the floral dress had dramatically changed the entire environment.

Philip was engrossed in a discussion about a recent sporting event with a young man sitting next to him. I outlined some local points of interest to a middle aged couple who I now understood were down from the country for tests and treatment and likely to be staying in Brisbane for two to three weeks. The previous deafening silence had been quickly replaced with animated chatter. If captured on film and shown without any hospital identifying features, we might well have appeared to be a group of travellers passing time in a bus station or a group of friends awaiting entry to an event.

I was stunned by the transformation, and my amazement reached dizzy new heights when some 15 minutes later, the receptionist called out a woman's name and our gorgeous, floral-clad friend interrupted her conversation with the teenage boy she had been engaging with for the past few minutes, and with a quick 'Oh, that's me,' followed the receptionist through the door that led to the scanning rooms. Her support person rearranged his oversized jacket and smiled in response to the kiss she blew him as she left the room. In all my speculations about who she might be and what her purpose was for being there, not in my wildest dreams could I have imagined that she was a patient!

The energy in the room, once changed, took on a whole new shape. As names were called and people disappeared, friendly comments of 'good luck' and 'see you soon' accompanied them as they followed the receptionist down towards the 'testing stations'.

Support people came and went, bearing trays of freshly brewed coffee and luscious cakes which were quickly distributed to the owners of the original orders. We'd moved from a group in isolated grief to a community engaged in mutual support.

Heaven forbid, we'd practically exchanged phone numbers and were about to start organising to spend Christmas together.

It was mid-afternoon and the coming and going of patients had been constant, as had been the trips to the coffee shop downstairs. Political discussions had been engaged in, current affairs had been discussed, new cancer treatments and insights shared and names and medical conditions exchanged. I was sitting next to the couple from out of town. The woman was living with a metastasised breast cancer. Her husband, a work-toughened farmer, looked weary and broken-hearted. I could see that her illness had been a long and arduous journey for him. She had made three trips to the scanning area and, from the information given to them by the radiologist, had one more set of scans to undergo before they could make their way to their hotel located a couple of blocks from the hospital.

A man in surgical scrubs strode confidently into the room and approached my new out of town friends. 'I've got some bad news, Mrs Smith,' he declared nonchalantly.

The room went silent. Mrs Smith was a friend now. We had all interacted with her at some level. We'd sipped coffee together. She had shared her carrot cake with the teenage boy opposite her. We were connected. Bad news for Mrs Smith was, by association, bad news for us. Mr Smith went pale. I felt compelled to reach out, and as I did, he took my hand. 'Surely,' I thought to myself, 'surely, you aren't going to tell her here in front of everybody?'

Mr Surgical Scrubs was undeterred by the imposing silence and the array of pleading, horror-stricken eyes and continued relentlessly. 'The scanner is malfunctioning and there will be approximately 15 minutes delay.'

The collective sigh of relief rattled around the walls and the ensuing burst of spontaneous laughter alerted Surgical Scrubs to the inappropriateness of his approach and his news. He glanced around the room, a blush rising rapidly to cover his neck and face. 'Guess that wasn't the best way to deliver that, was it?' He joined in the laughter and instantly became one of the group.

I often tell this story in workshops, especially when somebody voices an opinion that they, as an individual, don't make a difference. We all make a difference, in every situation we are in and every time we engage with others. And what I think this story really illustrates is that the difference we make can be either helpful or unhelpful, depending on what we choose to do.

The glorious woman in the floral dress had every reason to be dismal and dismayed, yet she chose to enter the room with a commitment to bringing joy and happiness. She succeeded big time.

Mr Surgical Scrubs, no doubt feeling busy and overwhelmed, forgot to choose his words or his approach well, and within seconds brought the energy down to an all-time low. With that one announcement, the energy in the room fell from light and connected to more desperate and panic-stricken than it had been early that morning when Philip and I had first arrived.

His capacity to see the impact and make amends restored the energy and swept him laughingly into the group. We were brothers and sisters in arms, and he was now part of our army.

As the saying goes, everybody makes a positive difference—some when they arrive, and some when they leave. I would add that our impact is always within our capacity to choose, and we shouldn't forget that situations can always be redeemed if we are prepared to notice and respond.

Carve out some time for yourself—no matter how impossible it seems

Philip's cancer was definitely making itself known now. Dr Maree had started to prescribe serious painkillers (class A equivalent—a dangerous, but potentially significant income stream should we have put them on the black market). The appearance of our fridge altered dramatically as more and more drugs took the space previously occupied by food.

The bone density treatment offered new additions to the accumulating side effects. For about two weeks after the treatment, Philip would experience significant bone aching and flu-like symptoms. The hormone treatment still rendered him temporarily paranoid, the radiation left him burnt and tired, and the introduction of stronger painkillers blurred his thinking and left him disorientated. Compared to all this, any symptoms being offered by the cancer were undetectable. It's an ironic situation. The disease itself is probably more bearable than the treatment. Without the treatment, however, Philip's life expectancy was very limited. We were caught in a medical catch 22 and it was not comfortable.

The hormone injections (a three monthly event) were being administered by a neighbour. Kent is a nurse who worked for some time in palliative care nursing. He proved to be an invaluable person to have around. Whenever I was concerned (which was frequently), I would call Kent, who would listen carefully to my sometimes hysterical explanation of the situation and then respond with one of the following:

1. That's normal. Try taking steps a, b or c.
2. OK, I'm on my way.
3. We need a doctor and I'm on my way.

Whatever the response, I instantly felt more in control, as I trusted Kent's assessment and felt confident that he would be there to help me if needed.

The bone density treatment was administered monthly at the chemo ward of the Prince Charles hospital in Chermside (a northern suburb of Brisbane). After the initial meltdown, I got more used to attending that ward with Philip. This was fortunate, because it was to become a place that we would spend a lot of time at in the future.

The radiation was given weekly at the Royal Brisbane Hospital and the oncology visits were at Holy Spirit Northside (adjoining the Prince Charles). Helen's chemotherapy was administered at the Wesley Hospital, and all her oncology visits were also there.

Sometimes their schedules would collide and I would find myself dropping off the first patient and picking up the second patient to take them somewhere else. I joked with both of them that if they had to get cancer together, couldn't they align their treatment so I only had one trip?

With all these hospital visits, the baby shawl was progressing nicely and was quite quickly finished, in plenty of time for the arrival of my first grandchild.

Work was still busy, and when I wasn't at medical appointments I was almost always at work. The farm feeding was fitted in around that. The only thing that I insisted was 'untouchable' was my Wednesday night horse riding. I was progressing with my show jumping and found that the only way you can safely put over 500 kilos of horse over several 90 centimetre jumps is to be one hundred percent focused on the task. My riding was my respite. There could be no cancer, no work, no family issues in the saddle with me. It was my hour a week, and it was sacred.

Laugh and (occasionally) live dangerously

Philip's second round of radiation seemed to have hit the spot, and he was able to reduce his painkillers quite significantly for a period of time. This resulted in the return of both his co-ordination and his lucidity. We felt like we'd hit the treatment jackpot.

The hormone injections and the bone density treatment continued and all indications were that both approaches were achieving our objectives. We resigned ourselves to the side effects, because the outcomes were worth it. Philip even became well enough to engage in many aspects of life unassisted again.

Helen was continuing with treatment and had incorporated the services of a homeopath. She placed great store in the homeopathies to support her body through the chemo, and I believe the combination of her faith in the practitioner and her sheer guts and determination enabled her to continue working and participating to some degree in life.

I continued to be her 'chemo buddy' and while these were incredibly difficult times, they were also beacons of closeness in my memories of Helen. The knitting project now complete, we spent the chemo hours in deep conversation, and when we needed lighter moments, in raucous laughter (usually inspired by some inane story in a popular magazine). My friendship with Helen had spanned some thirty-plus years, with the combined sum of four daughters between us and a divorce each. It was a deep and close friendship, and I felt honoured to be by her side during her final footsteps.

People often asked me why we didn't create a different strategy for Helen's treatment, given that I was so involved in Philip's. In fact, when her cancer returned for the third time, Helen originally banned me from participating on the grounds that I had enough to do. However, to not be there was unthinkable in my mind and amidst the horrendous rubble of hospitals and treatment cycles, there were wonderful gems of memories. Helen's dry and unfaltering sense of humour sustained us both through difficult days and, when her energy levels rose enough, we'd enjoy long coffee chats while languishing in sun-soaked deck chairs.

True friendship, to my mind, isn't a passing, fleeting fad. It's a true commitment. Sure, we all lose touch with people we were connected to in past, but I'm talking about that deep level of friendship that has played a major role in who we have become and what we do in life. For me, that level of friendship isn't taken lightly, and carries the same 'better or worse, in sickness and in health' vows as a marriage. Helen's illness was as much a part of our friendship as her health. From my perspective, there was no question about where I would be.

Philip's new-found health improvements saw him able to engage more fully in life. His flying was progressing, and he was close to achieving his lifelong dream of obtaining his pilot's licence. He was flying solo now, and spent most evenings engrossed in flight manuals and various other plane-related texts.

I had included some cross-country riding in my equestrian passion and was exploring and developing my own riding courage. I was riding in group classes and had bonded well with the others in my group. I felt well supported while in the saddle. The others knew of our story at home and they all worked hard to create a 'safe space' for me emotionally where I could release tensions if I needed to (generally by riding faster). They also encouraged my boundary pushing, getting very excited with me when I achieved a new milestone.

I vividly remember one such cross-country lesson. We'd started with some small jumps (logs) at the bottom of a hill. We'd all warmed up on the jumps, and then another rider and I 'caught' the same idea simultaneously and without any consultation, lined up a separate jump each and put our steeds at them. Once clear, we gave the horses their heads for a fast gallop up the hill. We reached the top within milliseconds of each other, both laughing and completely invigorated. I could feel Rocky's strong and solid frame, his own spirit lifted by the run. The summer breeze ruffled the strands of hair that had escaped from the confines of my safety helmet, and in that moment my whole being resonated with pure joy.

At the top of the hill, Ella looked at me, beaming. 'Again?' she invited.

'You betcha!' I replied, and we swung the horses round and headed back down towards the jumps.

'When you kids have finished, just let us know,' called the instructor. She knew what cobwebs were being swept away that day and she supported our fast and furious sweeping.

In any times of difficulty, it is essential that we capture and hold onto the moments of happiness. I truly believe that whatever is happening, there are still always opportunities for joy—the smile from the nurse in the chemo ward, the jokes about the article in the magazine, the taste of the cake carefully transported from the cafe below, the success of a new recipe and the exhilaration of a fast gallop.

We had reached another safe island. Helen was having better days with the support of the homeopathies. Philip was flying (literally and metaphorically) and I had found my bliss in the saddle.

To not have relished and delighted in that time would have been foolish. We all held fast to the respite and recharged our batteries in preparation for the next hurdle.

Say goodbye with love

I had made my daily call to Helen to check in on how things were, and suggested I pop over later with an evening meal for them all.

'I've just got to duck to the hospital,' she threw casually into the conversation. She used a similar tone to one she might use to mention popping down to the shops for bread and milk.

'Why?' I questioned cautiously, for Helen had made making light of things into an art form and I wasn't fooled by her casual approach.

'The stomach swelling won't go down, I'm really uncomfortable and they want to do scans. I'll just get a taxi. It'll be fine.'

Nothing felt 'fine' to me. 'I'm on my way,' I insisted. 'Don't go anywhere until I get there.' Without giving her a chance to protest, I hung up and got in the car.

Helen's stomach was severely distended, and she was clearly more than 'uncomfortable'. The car trip was a nightmare for her, as she desperately altered the seat position in a bid to find some degree of comfort. It must have felt like the longest car journey ever, and I was thankful that I'd interrupted her plan for a taxi by making the phone call.

She was admitted to hospital. I don't think either of us realised that this was to be her final admission. Scans showed extensive fluid retention and in subsequent days, the fluid was drained but kept rebuilding, almost faster than the draining process could manage it.

When I visited Helen a few days later, she had been moved to another floor. I realised that her new room was in the palliative care area, not the oncology area. Nobody had spoken to us about the imminence of her death, but the move of location said it louder than any medical person could have.

The following Wednesday, I was at the hospital with Helen. I had been with her most of the day and intended staying through the night. She was weak and in pain, emotionally and physically exhausted, frightened and fully aware of what was happening. Scans had been taken and there was an appointment with yet more specialists the next day to determine what steps could be taken to keep her comfortable. We were now beyond treatment and into comfort (the purpose of the palliative care area).

Helen looked tired and appeared pale and fragile against the white bed linen of the hospital bed. I sat in the chair next to her. Nothing much was being said. I guess we both knew we didn't need words; we were at a point far beyond words. Helen turned her head towards me. It hurt her to move even the slightest bit and I seethed in anger at the inadequacy of a medical system that still couldn't manage pain.

'Goodbye,' she whispered.

I looked over at her, panic-stricken and heard myself say 'What! Where are you going?' Said to anyone else at this time, this comment might have been deemed inappropriate, but I knew Helen, after all our years of friendship and multiple hours in treatment rooms and doctors surgeries, would see the compassion in the lightness.

'I'm not going anywhere,' she laughed. 'When that goodbye comes, it will a tad more emotional.'

A gentle silence hung between us for a couple of seconds—a silence that highlighted that 'death' had just been mentioned, and for the first time it had entered as a close and very tangible reality. We knew it, we'd known it for some weeks now, but we hadn't yet vocalised it. We both knew that 'that goodbye' wasn't far off but surely, I pleaded with the universe, not tonight, not yet, please.

'I said goodbye because you're going horse riding!' she exclaimed and I remember wondering where this sudden strength had come from.'

'N-n-no,' I stammered, 'not tonight. I can miss one night. I'm here with you, and here is where I want to be.'

'Yes, but it's not all about you,' she smiled. 'We've got a big day tomorrow, we both know that it's unlikely to be good news and I will need you to be strong and present. Right now, you are worn out and done in. An hour on a horse, a good sleep and you'll pick up, I know. I've seen it happen to you. So go away, I promise I'll be here tomorrow when you get back. Go horse riding, because I know if you do, you'll be better able to be here for me tomorrow.'

Her case made too much sense so I stood up, kissed her forehead, stroked her head, long since devoid of hair, and left. There were no words to say. She didn't need words and I didn't have words.

I headed home, donned a pair of jodhpurs, grabbed my helmet and raced out again. Philip's enquiry of 'how's Helen?' was met with a tearful wave of a helmet. He knew there were no words either. When I returned from riding, I headed straight for the shower, announced I would be back at the hospital with Helen early the next day and crawled into bed.

Helen was right. I did need to be on my game the next day. In difficult times, it's important to still do something you love, not just because it is good for you, but because it means you are more able to be there for the people who need you and who you want to be there for. Martyrdom got nobody anywhere. Avoid it at all costs!

Just a short week later, it was time for *that* goodbye. Ironically, I had come straight from the riding school. Dressed in jodhpurs and riding boots, I curled up beside Helen on the bed and held her tight. She played with my hair as she told me how much she loved me, how important our friendship had been and how much she valued all the hours we had shared. I responded with whispers of my appreciation and memories of the delights of our friendship. I murmured into the soft folds of her neck. The feel of her shoulder is still imprinted on my hand, the hospital smell still inhabits my nose, but mostly the snippets of over 30 years of shared friendship still play in my psyche like glorious memories from a favourite movie.

Cancer robs us of so much, but one of its precious gifts is warning. Even as I reflect on that most precious and heartbreaking of moments, I am so pleased that I was wearing the right clothes!

I wasn't there when Helen died. We said our goodbyes and I moved over to make the space for her precious daughters and a number of family members who had arrived from Melbourne.

I didn't need to be there when she died. I had been there when she lived, and I knew she wouldn't die alone. She would be surrounded by love and caring and she would die knowing how special she was.

I was at a 'business' meeting. It was 20% business and 80% pleasure. The other two meeting attendees were friends and we were developing some future business plans over a lovingly prepared lunch and delicious coffee. The spacious deck of the renovated old Queenslander in Hamilton provided a perfect venue for our meeting and our business planning and social catch-up had gone well.

It was a still September day, with perfect Brisbane weather. It was a day to be born (whether into this world or the next world) and I sat with my arm on the rail and admired the manicured gardens and the perfectly-tended picket fences. Without warning, my nostrils filled with the nausea-provoking hospital smell that I'd come to detest. A breeze, previously lacking, blew through my hair and I noticed with interest that while the smell and the breeze arrived simultaneously, not a plant or a blade of grass moved. As quickly as it came, it left. Someone beside me asked, 'Are you alright?'

'Helen just died,' I responded. The rail was suddenly replaced by loving arms, and I succumbed to the much needed friendship-filled hug.

Within minutes, my phone alerted me to a message 'Mum passed away peacefully a while ago. I'm sorry, Joan,' signed Helen's younger daughter. It was short, it was simple, it was without frills or elaboration. The inclusion of 'I'm sorry' recognised the closeness of the friendship Helen and I had shared and, to me, highlighted how wonderfully Helen had raised and nurtured her daughters. It also marked the end of an amazing life and an incredible journey of courage.

I had nowhere to go. Philip had organised a work meeting at our place and I wasn't up to going home and facing people. When I left Hamilton, I meandered for ages in the car, turning up streets just because they were there and driving along the river. Finally, I decided I needed to head towards home. I stopped on the way at a saddlery and bought a pair of jodhpurs. It seems silly now that I'm writing it, but it was all I could think of to do.

I had let Philip know of Helen's passing and he had wound the meeting up as quickly as he could to clear the space for me to come home. That night we sat in silence. I wished I'd made lamb pie for dinner, though I know I wouldn't have eaten it. It was too early for stories of Helen. As the evening wore on, Philip glanced over at me and said, 'Well, she found out first.'

'What?' I enquired.

'What happens when you die,' he replied. 'Helen and I talked about it a lot. She's found out first. We wondered which one of us would.'

Helen and I had a remarkable friendship based on time and events, whereas Helen and Philip had an incredible connection based on circumstance and understanding. A significant point of our triangle had just disappeared and the resulting void was shapeless.

It was a painful hole that projected a scary future, because doctors had been clear that Philip was far from out of the woods.

Be stronger than you look (or feel)

The air in the funeral home felt heavy and close. I sat on a bench at the back of the room and watched in silence as people filed in. Some faces I knew, others I didn't. Despite being some days after Helen's passing, it still seemed too surreal that she was gone. I was far from accepting it. I kept expecting to hear her voice, her laughter, 'gotcha, you fools!' ringing out across the gathering crowd.

People sauntered past me, some resting a hand gently on my shoulder as they passed by. My stomach was churning. Grief is painful—physically painful.

It was so hard to come to terms with the fact that Helen was gone. Her body lay in the box at the front of the room. Her smiling face stared out at the crowd from an 8x10 photo frame. She looked so healthy and well in the photo. How could she possibly be dead?

Helen had made hats into a creative passion. She made several for herself through each round of chemo and wore them proudly in place of her hair. One of her hats sat on the coffin next to the photo.

Her girls looked tiny and frail, yet with eyes that had matured immensely through pain. They had old eyes in young bodies. Their eyes had seen too much.

The funeral director materialised, and I heard him ask about the coffin bearers. I stood up and moved towards him, and he looked at me in a surprised, almost judging way. Another woman, a relative of Helen's, also shifted towards the funeral director. There were four men to make up the six required for the procession. I saw the undertaker whispering to the men.

'They'll be fine,' I heard Philip say. 'Don't worry'. The undertaker looked at me and the other woman again and a slight shake of his head was only just discernible. He decided to check for himself and spoke directly to us.

'The coffin is very heavy.' His voice was low and soft. I heard his concern, but Philip was right, he didn't need to worry.

'I'm a lot stronger than I look,' I murmured, aware that my 150 centimetre frame and 50 kilo body weight didn't inspire much confidence in him.

He called the men over. 'The women go at the front,' he said. 'There is slightly less weight there.' With that, he took on an air of enhanced officiousness and strode across the room.

The service was about to start. Philip took my hand, and together we found a seat on the left hand side, a few rows from the front. Not quite family, but more than acquaintances. Every stage of our lives is governed by formalities and expectations, and funerals are no different.

I played nervously with the piece of paper in my hand. I'd sat alone the night before and made some notes. They were memories of a lifetime of friendship, and somehow they had successfully squeezed themselves onto one sheet of A4 paper. I didn't really need notes for my tribute to Helen. My heart held everything I wanted to say, but I didn't trust my heart. It was broken, and it wasn't fair to put more pressure on it.

I heard my name and felt Philip's nudge, and I moved robot-like towards the front of the room. From there I let my glance drift across the room, taking in the faces—people I hadn't seen for some time, people I'd never seen before and people I knew well. I looked up to the ceiling. 'You there, mate?' I enquired mentally, and a soft gentle ripple danced lightly down my spine. 'Ok then, let's go,' and I took my position at the lectern, put my A4 page down in front of me, took a deep breath, opened my mouth and brought forth a range of stories and memories—straight from my heart.

There was a mix of laughter and sadness, shared sporting achievements, boozy dinners out, getting lost on driving adventures, cooking successes and failures. There were endless stories, wonderful, glorious, happy stories and as I finished, I looked over at the 8x10 photo positioned on the coffin and I swear I saw Helen wink. It may have been my imagination, but I also think the hat moved ever so slightly.

'Farewell,' I whispered. 'See you on the other side.'

The coffin was heavy. Bloody heavy. The undertaker hadn't exaggerated. 'Jesus,' I thought as the supports were removed and it was left to six human arms to take the weight. I took a deep breath and started walking. It could have been ten times heavier and we would still have carried it. As soon as we exited the front door of the funeral home, four burly men came over to help. I remember one of them gently prising my fingers off the handle. I'd locked my hand tight.

At some point, we all adjourned back to Helen's for drinks. Philip and I went for a brief time, but we couldn't stay long. He had a radiation appointment that night and we needed to get to the hospital.

Cancer's dance doesn't even pause for funerals; the steps just go on and on and on.

Look for the koala in the trees

Philip's request to the universe to send him a koala for reassurance provided a whole range of new observation possibilities and some very interesting events.

As his cancer progressed, the testing regime was stepped up. After each bout of the different treatments there was invariably another round of some sort of tests. Whether it was blood tests to check PSA or scans to check the status of tumours, it seemed we were regularly engaged in either going for tests or waiting for results.

On one particular morning, Philip was getting ready for an appointment with Dr James when Rosie and Harry set off a chorus of barking that had us both rushing for the back door to investigate what was happening. They weren't excessively barky dogs, but neither of them was shy about informing us of some interesting visitor or an animal out of its enclosure.

I remember being woken up one morning by loud barking outside the bedroom window only to come face to face with a horse when I went to investigate. Mungie (who was staying at the farm with us for a while) had come through the fence during the night. Having spent a few good hours in the orchard, he had decided it was breakfast time and had come up to the house to pick up his food. Rosie and Harry were beside themselves with concern that said horse was not in his paddock and Rosie had no hesitation letting me know with some vigorous head shaking that the object of their vocal alert was standing right behind her and he was big!

Both dogs had been similarly noisy when Jesus and Eeyore had found a path out of the back of the property one day. In fact, almost like an excited crowd at a parade, the dogs had 'cheered' the donkeys home. Just as I was starting to despair at how I was going to round up two donkeys and bring them back across three properties, lo and behold, both escapees came sauntering down the road and arrived (hungry and ready for dinner) at the front gate to a very loud canine welcome.

So on this particular morning when the barking started, both Philip and I assumed we had another animal loose and went out prepared to apprehend the culprit and return whoever it was to his or her rightful abode.

Imagine our surprise when we located the source of the excitement and it an adult male koala, sitting at eye level in the tree right near the back door. Having successfully alerted us to the presence of our visitor, Rosie and Harry quickly lost interest in the whole thing and returned to their day beds for some well-earned rest.

Philip took the appearance of the koala very seriously. He was seeing Dr James that day to discuss the latest PSA results and his confidence that the results would be good instantly soared. True to his prediction, the results that day were very pleasing.

The pattern continued for the next couple of years. On test result day Philip would check the tree, and on many occasions our koala (now named Kelvin) would be sitting there happily to greet us. On each of the days of a visit from Kelvin, the test results were always good. At other times, Kelvin would be missing. Philip searched the gum trees around the property, but to no avail. On these days, the test results were always difficult.

It became a faultless pattern. Kelvin meant good results, no Kelvin, not so good results. It seems the universe had taken Philip's suggestion and was happily working with him on the 'koala indicator'.

Party hard, fly high and make plans

Another new year cruised in; however, this year marked my 50th birthday. I'm not one to be worried about numbers, but I do relish a good birthday celebration. I have always maintained that one day isn't enough and have managed to stretch each birthday out a bit longer each year. For the past few years my birthday had been celebrated for the entire month of March, and I saw no reason why this milestone should not enjoy at least that duration.

Philip suggested a big party, but I wasn't really up for that. The cost and the work of getting it together felt quite daunting. Money continued to leave the household like water down an endless drain and, while I don't want to sound mean, I was being particularly cautious. I suggested maybe we could plan a few little things that wouldn't stretch the budget too much more than it was already stretched and wouldn't take too much organising. I wasn't sure that either of us had the energy to pull together a big party.

Philip had other ideas. He contacted some friends, and together they formed a working party. I was informed that there would be a party and that I didn't have to do anything. I was also advised to be prepared for surprises.

The first surprise came a few days before the actual anniversary of the day I was born, when Philip returned from the airport in a state of excitement, waving a piece of paper in my face. Said piece of paper quickly revealed itself to be a pilot's licence. He had been working day and night at the theory and flying as much as he could to ensure that he could take me flying for my birthday. It was delivered as a *fait accompli*. I WAS going flying for my birthday. Luckily, I'm a tad adventurous, and I figured being Philip's first passenger couldn't be that dangerous, surely.

So the actual day arrived and we embarked on a morning flight, leaving Redcliffe Airport (to the north of Brisbane) and flying up the coast and returning across the mountains. It was glorious.

My afternoon was spent on a horse in the jumping arena. I felt like I'd had my share of birthday excitement.

The following Saturday night, the working party produced an amazing party and, once again, our home was filled with laughter and fun. The *piece de résistance* was an amazing carousel cake, complete with dancing horses and decorated in my favourite colours.

The event was videoed and friends left loving messages that were captured by the camera for all time. It was a glorious celebration and again, provided a wonderful oasis for us to rest near. Despite all that had happened, for that time of celebrations life felt good and truly worth celebrating.

Philip rallied for the party. Always in his element with a microphone in his hand, he relished the role of Master of Ceremonies, and the party was a successful blend of well-organised spontaneity. Enough was organised to ensure success, but there was plenty of room for improvisation.

Watching the video later, it was hard to believe that things would go downhill so quickly and that we were only a few short months away from some very difficult times. It's good that we don't know these things in advance, because if we did, the future would constantly rob us of the present. March 2005 provided so many magical moments that I would have hated to relinquish any of them to the future.

The radiation cycle had been completed sometime previously, and Philip had done well for some months. There were signs of pain returning and Dr Maree had responded with more scans and reintroduced the painkillers. The scans were showing that the tumours in the spine were once again active.

More radiation wasn't believed to be a good idea. As another option, Dr Maree outlined for us some pleasing results with a new chemo mix. Doctors had just started using the cocktail for prostate cancer and the results were good enough to justify the side effects. Once again, it was emphasised that it was unlikely that the chemo would a represent a cure; however, it was reasonable to expect that it offered us some time.

In the absence of any other alternatives, and with scans showing a distinct progression of the cancer, we elected to try the chemo. The commencement of Philip's chemo and my 50th birthday almost collided.

The much-worked-for pilot's licence was suddenly in jeopardy as the Civil Aviation Safety Authority deemed the increase in Philip's PSA, coupled with the commencement of chemotherapy, to present a significant risk. Philip received notice that he could only occupy the pilot's seat if he had a licensed pilot next to him.

This was a big blow for him. He had worked hard to achieve this dream and had held it for such a short time.

The chemo left him tired and nauseous, and to this day I'm not convinced it actually slowed the cancer. Still, it was a decision we had made at the time and we stuck to it and completed the suggested cycle.

The Thursday before Easter 2005 presented a major challenge. As I've mentioned, all of Philip's treatment options created fairly difficult side effects. All were on different time cycles, but it was only a matter of time before those cycles aligned. This happened on that particular Thursday.

Philip was scheduled for his hormone injection, his bone density treatment and his chemotherapy all on the same day. The hospital organised for it all to be administered, sequentially, during the same visit. They warned us that it would be an extra-long visit. My concerns were more focused on the potential for an exponential side effect blow out, and I was very nervous.

We were facing four days of public holidays and an unknown impact of the drug mix in his body. I firmly believed we needed a strategy.

We recruited some help from friends, and our agreed strategy was that if things escalated to a point that I couldn't cope, I'd call the nominated people and they would either come and take Philip home with them or come and stay with me to help (the final strategy being determined by the actual situation).

We nervously arrived at the hospital for our appointment. Throughout the variety of treatments, I gave Philip Reiki, which he found relaxing and, we both believed, offered some capacity to help.

The treatment over, we were discharged as day visitors and sent home to see what the chemical bomb might explode into.

It's always good to have a strategy. I believe it's much better to have a strategy you don't need than need a strategy you haven't got. I was armed with phone numbers, our nominated friends rang on our return home to check in, and we waited. We waited, and waited and absolutely nothing happened!

The impact of the combined treatments appeared to have cancelled out ALL the side effects. Philip hadn't been so well, so relaxed, so energetic and so healthy since before the diagnosis. 'Let's do the 'big hit' every time,' I suggested, but Dr Maree, though clearly very pleased about our experience, reminded us that the different cycles weren't conducive to that approach at all.

I've never done the mathematics to work out how frequently that treatment phenomenon might occur, I just know that Philip didn't get to experience the event again.

Make more plans

Out of the blue, Philip decided that he wanted to go on a holiday. I was enthused about the idea but somewhat scared about how we'd manage it. He completely terrified me when he insisted that he wanted to go to Stradbroke Island.

Straddie (as it is known colloquially), had been a favourite haunt of ours for years. Long, lazy weekends on the island and deliciously restful weeks in the sand had been significant parts of our relationship since we first connected.

Philip's insistence on going to Straddie was understandable, but with his health in the precarious place it had reached, I was not enthusiastic about holing away on an island for seven potentially pain-filled days. Dr Maree agreed wholeheartedly with me and tried hard to talk Philip out of it. 'There are no suitable medical facilities Philip.'

Philip remained resolved.

'I don't think this is fair to Joan.' Dr Maree played her ace card.

Philip responded with, 'Joan will be fine.'

I suggested the Sunshine Coast as an alternate destination. It had a glorious strip of stunning beaches well serviced by hospitals and reassuringly part of the mainland. Philip remained adamant. We were going to Straddie, and Harry and Rosie were coming as well. Eventually, I conceded defeat and set about organising an emergency evacuation plan.

Having our beautiful puppies along with us was very exciting. Straddie is a dog haven. The island welcomes its canine visitors and our many previous trips with the dogs confirmed for us that they enjoyed an island getaway just as much as we did. Harry's excitement whenever he arrived at the mainland ferry terminal was undeniable. (Rosie found the boat crossing somewhat distressing and would only participate if she was allowed to sit in my lap for the entire journey.) Once arrived at the island paradise, Harry always almost knocked himself out trying to jump out of a closed car window as we passed the off-leash dog-friendly beach.

He invariably showed great impatience when we insisted on finding and settling into our accommodation before Rosie, he and I embarked on the first of our mandatory twice daily long walks. Coming from a rural property, the dogs found a suburban-sized block somewhat constricting, so beach holidays included regular walks, irrespective of the weather. I estimated that the dogs and I perambulated approximately 30 kilometres per day. It was healthy exercise for all of us.

Dr Maree's note about the lack of medical facilities concerned me greatly. Straddie offered the services of local doctor, but there was no significant medical facility and certainly nothing that resembled a hospital. Philip's health was precarious to say the least, and his treatment regime was intensive and involved a range of potential side effects that also needed to be managed.

Further, we knew nobody on the island to whom we could turn for assistance or support so, in terms of managing Philip's needs and his health requirements, I was most definitely going to be on my own.

In the spirit of my *better to have a strategy you don't need than need a strategy you haven't got* philosophy, prior to heading off the island I ensured we had a 'getting Philip to medical attention' plan ready to activate.

Having the dogs with us represented both a joy and, in the event that we needed to get Philip back to the mainland in a hurry, a challenge. The quickest way off the island was by helicopter (which clearly wouldn't be able to also transport two Border Collies), with the second option being by commercially-operated speedboat (again, not really canine friendly). Obviously, I couldn't just leave the dogs unattended on the island. In addition, both of the quick options meant that we wouldn't have a vehicle on the other side for transportation. (The only option for returning with the vehicle was the vehicular ferry that transported us over.)

I put the word out and, as always, friends came flocking to our assistance. A strategy materialised quickly. In the event of an incident, I would ring a friend who lived close to the speedboat arrival point. She would transport Philip directly to hospital. I would follow on the ferry with the dogs. Another friend would meet me off the ferry to take Harry and Rosie, allowing me to go straight on to the hospital.

We boarded the ferry for our island holiday with a kaleidoscopic mix of emotions. Philip was incredibly nostalgic. For him, this was a farewell journey. As anticipated, Harry was beside himself with excitement, a black and white mass of slobbering tongue and wagging tail. Rosie, somewhat apprehensive about the ferry ride, was mustering all her bravery as she knew the destination was well worth the trip. I was terrified and unbelievably sad. Both Philip and I knew this was almost certainly our last trip across to the island together and I was pleased to have our canine carers to help support and distract us as we prepared to retrace some wonderfully romantic steps and close some powerfully important cycles.

Straddie welcomed us with a perfect island morning. The sun hung low in the spotless blue sky. A gentle breeze set the trees in a united wave as we passed, and the glorious smell of the ocean guided us towards Point Lookout. Accommodation keys in hand, we made our way to the familiar beach house where we'd spent countless long weekends and many wonderful holiday weeks. Harry and Rosie, familiar with these tranquil surroundings, raced from the car to the back garden of the house.

Within minutes, Rosie had lazily established herself on the outside day bed facing the ocean. If she'd called out an order for a gin and tonic I wouldn't have been one bit surprised. Harry, by far the more active of the two, had his lead firmly grasped between his teeth and diligently followed us back and forth as we unpacked the car. He was sending us a clear message. 'Stuff the unpacking, let's go for a walk!'

However, even the perfection of the day and the excitement of the moment couldn't dilute the overwhelming sense of foreboding that followed me as I diligently filed groceries in the allocated cupboards, positioned bags and made up the bed.

Philip, exhausted from the trip, immediately went for a lie down. Having ensured he was settled and as comfortable as possible, finally, to Harry's delight, I took off with the dogs for a long walk around Point Lookout, culminating in a joyous, freedom-filled run along the off-leash beach.

Know that the best-laid plans ...

The days passed steadily. Philip's energy levels were low and he was rarely out of bed for more than ten minutes at a time. My daily routine quickly settled into a set series of activities. On rising, I'd get some breakfast for Philip and make myself a cup of tea. Once Philip was resettled, I would head off with the dogs for our morning walk, featuring a coffee stop at the cafe in Point Lookout. The dogs would happily wait for me as I sipped my caffeine hit and took in the ocean views from the front deck of the cafe.

Each of the twice daily walks would finish at the off-leash beach. I enjoyed a steady jog along the sand and Harry and Rosie burnt up any residual energy by running back and forth, usually successfully completing at least four or five times the distance I had managed.

We would return suitably exercised, and I would help Philip with bathing and offer some morning tea (which he would generally take with Rosie on the day bed). He would then return to bed and I would set about some writing. In the week we were on Straddie I completed about 50% of the first draft of a novel. It is a piece of work that lies untouched to this day. Somehow, the will to go back to it has never returned.

On some days, Philip felt well enough to try a light lunch, though generally he slept through, waking up in time for an early dinner, after which the dogs and I would do our second walk/run for the day.

This was to become quite a routine for us. On about day four, Sue-Ellen rang to check in.

'How's it going, kiddo?'

'It's interesting,' I replied. 'Lots of walking with the dogs, morning coffee overlooking the ocean and I'm writing with gay abandon. It could almost be a perfect holiday except that Philip is going downhill, and every moment I'm reminded that we might have very little time left'.

The sadness in her sigh said it all. 'Look after you,' she instructed. After we hung up, I reflected on my daily activities and concluded that, in essence, that was exactly what I was doing.

Each day saw the gathering of a few more clouds. Straddie is notorious for its storms and they are amazingly powerful and awe-inspiring events. We watched as the weather got heavier and heavier, but we could never have anticipated the intensity it was building up to or the health crisis that was building up in Philip in perfect unison with the weather. The true meaning of 'perfect storm' was about to be revealed to us.

When the heavens finally opened, they were fuelled by gale force winds and thunder and lightning that, with the backdrop of the ocean, could only be described as monumental. About an hour into the storm, Philip collapsed with kidney pain.

All transport services on and off the island had been halted. There was no ferry, no speedboat, and most definitely no helicopter.

My worst fears about this holiday were being realised. We were isolated, we had no phones (all communication had shut down), visibility outside was less than an arm's length in front of you, making driving the twisting roads along the cliff tops totally treacherous, and Philip was rapidly going downhill. In the painful fog that he was experiencing he had lost the capacity for speech and was reduced to a moaning, writhing mass on the bedroom floor. I had no idea what to do and no-one to call on for help.

I decided we needed to be ready to evacuate as soon as the storm passed and busied myself packing up our things and lining them up at the front door. I prepared text messages to send to the help crew and had them ready to transmit when phone reception returned. Breaking the rules of the house rental, I brought the dogs inside to wait out the storm with us. Harry immediately went to Philip's side and lay beside him and Rosie curled up with me in the corner of the room where I could watch Philip's chest to ensure he was still breathing.

'Please don't die here,' I pleaded with him. 'Please hang in there until I can get help.' My voice was screaming in my head, 'please, please, please!' The sound of my own begging was even louder than the storm. Rosie snuggled up close. I swear at one point, she even put her paws around my neck and cuddled me. I was terrified. I was too terrified to cry; all I could do was hold on to Rosie and beg Philip to stay alive.

And then, finally, the winds dropped, the thunder and lightning stopped and the rain started to ease. It was 2.00 am and the storm had raged for over six hours. Philip had fallen into a fitful sleep on the floor and his groaning had lessoned. Harry, his head on Philip's back (right around the kidney area), looked at me sadly. The 'perfect storm' had impacted enormously on all of us and none of us were at all worried about the weather.

I started getting things into the car and was on my third trip when Philip started to sit up. 'What's happening?' he enquired.

'We're leaving,' I explained, picking up another bundle of belongings and heading towards the door.

'It's the middle of the night!' he exclaimed. 'What's the problem?'

As it turned out, he had no recollection of the pain or the storm. Perplexed about why he was on the floor, he sat up and started playing with Harry's ears.

'I'm feeling okay,' he said. 'I think we should stay.'

He got up, brushed his teeth and got into bed. He was fast asleep within a few minutes.

I unpacked the car for the second time for this holiday. Rather than packing everything away in cupboards and drawers again, I stacked most the bags in the entry hall, taking time to put any perishable items in the fridge and crawled into bed. Rosie and Harry, again against all the rules of the house rental, curled up on the end of our bed and quickly went to sleep. I lay wide awake for some time, waiting impatiently for my heart rate to return to something that might resemble 'normal'.

Sunshine streamed through the window the following morning and Philip was up and ready for breakfast early.

'I think we should go to the beach today,' he said. 'Maybe do some four wheel driving. What do you think?'

His pain levels eased to manageable for the rest of the holiday. Scans taken on our return revealed well-established tumours in both of his kidneys.

Acknowledge that you can't see into the future—which is probably just as well

We were into the hard yards now. Philip's mobility was severely impacted as his pain levels increased and the subsequent pain management drugs were ramped up. He continued to attend Geoff Wilson's political office one day a week, but I'm not sure how effective he was able to be.

One particular Friday early in December 2005, I returned home from running a workshop with the Queensland Department of Health. The training room we were using was located in a building directly opposite the Royal Brisbane Hospital and for the entire day I had a full view of the hospital, little knowing that I would be spending the night there.

Philip hadn't arrived when I reached home and I started to get concerned when he hadn't turned up an hour or so later. There was no answer when I tried his mobile phone, and I worked hard to calm myself with the thought that maybe he'd stayed for Friday drinks (an unlikely reality at this point, as he was always exhausted by the end of the day). My sigh of relief when I heard the car pull into the driveway was quickly silenced when I saw how he was.

His 'walking' had taken on the appearance of a humanoid crab. He seemed reliant on support and stopped regularly to hold onto something. I watched in horror as he half crawled, half shuffled into the house.

'What's happening?' My voice betrayed my attempt to sound confident. 'Are you in pain?'

We had established an agreement some time previously, that if the pain levels became difficult, he would come home. A part of me was irritated that he had stayed on at work in such a clearly challenging state. The irritation was, however, minimal compared to my concern.

'I think I'm becoming paralysed,' he stated, his face full of terror.

My heart stopped; I'm sure my heart just stopped. I stood in shock, not knowing what to do or what to say. Dr Maree had warned us that at least one of the tumours presented a risk of spinal compression. Despite the two rounds of radiation and the subsequent chemotherapy, this rogue tumour just kept growing. Located just below the base of his neck, it was slowly compressing his spinal cord.

I rang her office and spoke to her locum (Dr Maree was away on a much deserved break). I explained as best I could who we were and what the situation appeared to be and the locum suggested I drive Philip to the Prince Charles Hospital, where he could be assessed.

The paralysis was advancing rapidly, and while Philip had been able to crab his way up the driveway to get to the house, he practically needed to be carried back to the car. Between us, we got him to the vehicle and I drove to the hospital. The car practically knew its own way to the Prince Charles Hospital by now, which was good, because I'm not sure how I drove there. Somehow, we made it.

On arrival at casualty, I parked right outside the door and raced in to get assistance. Philip had deteriorated significantly during the drive and our half carry/half walk approach to get him in the car was no longer viable. He now needed to be carried. The orderly grabbed a wheelchair and together we got Philip into it and into the emergency room.

The locum had sent word to the emergency ward that we were coming and a doctor was waiting to assess the situation. Within minutes he came back to see me. 'He needs to be at the Royal Brisbane,' he said. 'This situation is life threatening and we don't have the facilities to manage it. He needs to be transported now'.

The thought of another drive was terrifying, I asked about an ambulance. 'I can call you one,' the doctor replied, 'but because you are at a hospital, you won't get priority. It will be considered that you are in medical care and therefore it won't be considered an emergency. On a Friday night, you could wait for hours for an ambulance, and your husband doesn't have hours.'

The orderly helped me get Philip back into the car. I put myself into some sort of robotic trance. All I knew was that I had to get Philip from Chermside to the Royal Brisbane Hospital, during peak hour on a Friday night, and I had to do it quickly. I was completely, mind-numbingly terrified.

The phone rang. It was Sue-Ellen. 'Hey buddy, how are you?'

'Philip's paralysed. We're on our way to the RBH.'

'In an ambulance?'

'No, I'm driving. We haven't got time to wait for an ambulance.'

'Be careful.' She rang off.

I pulled the car to a screeching halt outside the emergency ward of the RBH and landed my hand on the horn. I assume that the Prince Charles had rung because an orderly appeared with a wheelchair and together we got Philip into the admissions area. I had no idea whether my car was in a parking zone or not. I didn't give two hoots whether they towed it or trashed it; I was beyond caring about such things. The world was crashing down around me, the walls of my life were coming in, I could hear screaming and it was mine. It was echoing in my head, silent to the outside world, but deafening inside my skull. I ran with the wheelchair into the emergency ward. There waiting for us was Sue-Ellen.

'You're not doing this one alone, kiddo,' she said and tagged on beside me. When the admissions nurse looked at us and asked what our relationship to Philip was, I answered 'I'm his wife' and Sue-Ellen added immediately 'And I'm her sister.' 'Good' said the nurse, 'Family only, I'm afraid. We're crazy busy in there.' We entered the chaotic world of the biggest emergency room in Brisbane on a Friday night.

For what seemed like hours, doctors kept coming over and sticking pins in Philip's torso and legs. With every examination, the paralysis had spread and at 11.00 pm on that horrible Friday night his paralysis was declared 'complete'. He was officially a quadriplegic.

A lovely Asian doctor had been in attendance since we arrived, and with every visit to Philip he stopped to spend time with me. His generosity of time in a space that resembled a war zone was commendable, and I'm sad that I can't remember his name because he deserves recognition.

Just before midnight, he came and took me aside. 'We're taking him to a ward,' he said. 'There is a neurological team on the way; I'm not sure what's going to happen. I'm going to come up with you and I'll stay with you until the neuro team arrives.' It was now after midnight and with the migration up to the ward imminent, Sue-Ellen held me close for several minutes, told me to call her if I needed anything at all and headed off home. The rest of us made our way towards the lifts, and I was totally aware that this could be a one way journey.

When the neurosurgeon arrived, she looked refreshed and wide awake. If I hadn't known that she'd just been woken up and summoned to the hospital, I'd have sworn that she had been waiting round the corner, fixing her makeup in anticipation of being hailed to perform major surgery. She quickly went through the hospital notes, asked a series of questions, stuck the mandatory pins in Philip's legs and then motioned for me to speak to her outside.

'It's not good,' she said 'If he were an older man, I'd do nothing and let nature take its course. Without intervention, it is unlikely he will be alive in the morning. However, he is young and I see a small window of possibility. I'd like your permission to operate to see if we can relieve the pressure on his spine.' She looked at me searchingly.

'That's not my decision,' I answered. 'That's Philip's call'.

We returned to the ward together and the neurosurgeon went through the details of her suggested action with Philip. She was frank and to the point (which Philip would have appreciated) and she outlined that, with the surgery she was suggesting, his chances of survival were very slim and his chances of ever moving his legs again were pretty much zero. Without the surgery he would be lucky to have a few more hours. 'What do you want me to do, Philip?' she asked.

'Do we have to operate now?' he queried.

'Yes, it's 1.00 in the morning, Philip and I'm standing here with my handbag. If I thought you had any chance of surviving more than a couple of hours, I'd be catching up on my sleep. We have to go now if we're going.'

'Start scrubbing, doc.' His attempt at lightness was admirable, but his shaking voice let him down horribly.

The neurosurgeon left immediately, advising a nurse who had just magically appeared (or maybe was there all the time but I hadn't noticed her) to get the team ready. The lovely Asian doctor, who had been waiting near the window of the ward, stepped forward.

'I'll leave you two alone,' he said to me. 'This is very risky surgery. You need to say goodbye just in case.'

I can't remember what I said; that moment is gone from my memory. I just remember Philip looking at me and saying 'thank you'—no details, no elaboration, just 'thank you'.

The Asian doctor was waiting just outside the door as they wheeled Philip out and he suggested I go home. 'The operation will take hours and we have nowhere comfortable for you to wait. I promise I'll ring as soon as I know anything. Go home and lie down.' In some sort of robotic trance, that is just what I did.

I had, of course, contacted Philip's children, and when I got home his daughter was there to wait out the surgery with me. I lay on the bed and waited for the phone to ring. When it did, it was the lovely Asian doctor again. 'The surgery is done and Philip is in recovery. Come back whenever you can.' His voice was soft and caring.

'How did it go?' I asked, hoping to hear that a miracle had occurred and everything was fixed, including the cancer.

'I don't know. You'll need to speak to the surgeon when you get here, but I do know that he has survived the surgery and that is a big hurdle overcome.'

'Our' Asian doctor was waiting for me when we got back. By my calculations he had done at least a 12 hour shift. 'Don't you go home?' I asked him.

'Yes, eventually,' he said. 'We were very busy last night and I wanted to see this case through.'

All Philip's children had arrived at the hospital and their faces revealed their pain. I was relieved to have the family around me. The events of the night before still seemed surreal and having the others there was a helpful anchor—for us all, I felt.

The hospital staff positioned us outside intensive care, explaining that Philip would be transferred there as soon as he was stabilised enough to move, and then we would then be able to see him. We waited impatiently. When my phone rang, revealing an unknown number, I nearly didn't answer it. I didn't feel up to conversations with anybody, and especially someone whose number wasn't in my phone. However, automatic reaction took over and answered the phone on my behalf.

'Joan?' enquired an unfamiliar voice.

'Yes,' I responded despondently.

The caller went on to identify herself as one of the nurses in the recovery ward. 'Philip's doing really well,' she advised, 'and we're bypassing intensive care. It could be a few hours before we can get him onto the ward though, so I'm making arrangements to get you into recovery. We don't usually let family in, but we're pretty quiet and we all think you need to see him. It's just you though, sorry. The others can see him when we get him to the ward. There is somebody on their way to get you, see you soon.'

Yet another nurse materialised in front of me and I marvelled at the medical profession's capacity to emulate the 'beam me up Scotty' transportation of *Star Trek*. The kids all went to get themselves a drink and I followed the magically appearing nurse to recovery. To my amazement, there was Philip sitting up in bed, eating ice-cream and swapping jokes with the nursing staff. 'Do you know what sort of night we've had?' I joked with him as I accepted a lick of his Magnum Classic.

'Yeah, sorry about that,' he mumbled. 'Hey, lift the end of the bedclothes. I've got a surprise for you.'

I duly lifted the bedclothes and witnessed both his feet moving, including all ten toes wiggling.

'That's great!' I exclaimed, surprised, as we had been warned that this outcome was pretty much impossible.

'I know,' he replied. 'I'm going to be fine. So much for quadriplegic, hey?'

The recovery nurse called me over to the nurses' station and handed me the phone. 'The surgeon would like to speak with you,' she invited.

'How's he doing?' enquired a voice I'd only known for about eight hours but which was unbelievably familiar already.

'Great,' I answered. 'He's moving his feet'.

'That's fantastic.' She hesitated slightly. 'But Joan, I've just been in his back. Philip is never walking again. His spinal cord is irreparably damaged. You have a long road ahead of you, wheelchair adjustment, it'll be months before he comes home. I'll see you later today when he's on the ward.'

'What'd the doc say?' was Philip's immediate enquiry when I returned to his bedside.

'She said that's fantastic,' I shared, deliberately omitting the rest of the conversation. After all, why spoil his ice-cream?

As it turned out, that omission was probably the best thing I could have done.

Appreciate all miracles

By 2.00 pm that afternoon, Philip was settled into the spinal care ward. Surrounded by motorbike accident victims and people who had fallen from great heights, he almost looked like a fraud (no traction, no monitoring machines). He certainly acted as if he didn't belong there. He seemed in pretty good spirits, engaging in banter with anybody who ventured into his room.

The afternoon disappeared into a haze of discussions with doctors, lots more sombre looks and horrendous forecasts regarding the journey ahead for Philip. The neurosurgeon held fast to her prediction that Philip was now permanently quadriplegic; however, she felt she had been successful in saving his life. He was facing months of rehabilitation and, with the cancer now rampant in his system, the fact that he might never come home was glaringly apparent to me. I was left wondering if we had done the humane thing by putting him through this massive surgery.

As the afternoon progressed, a medical team gathered outside his room and after yet more discussions and another round of sombre faces, the group (including quite a collection of student doctors), entered the ward looking very official with clipboards in hand and stethoscopes dangling from their necks.

On Philip's insistence, the surgeon ceremoniously lifted the bed clothes to reveal his feet, whereupon he immediately lifted his left foot and placed it carefully in her hand. She literally reeled backwards in shock. 'That's not all,' teased Philip, and promptly lifted his right foot to join in the fun.

'Get me a physio,' requested the surgeon and waved her eyebrows at me to meet her outside.

'That's impossible,' she gasped. 'Every medical book I've ever read says that is impossible. His spinal cord is damaged—this shouldn't happen.'

'But it has', I shrugged my shoulders.

'Yes, and we're going with it, I'll have a physio look at him and let's start planning to get him up—probably not until Monday, though that will be the physio's call.'

We returned to the room. 'Well, Philip,' she looked at him, a huge smile lighting up her face, 'I have never been so happy to be wrong. It looks like you may walk again after all.'

'Well, doc,' he replied. 'My theory is, when a doctor says you'll end up quadriplegic, you just can't take that news sitting down.' The laughter in the room was awkward and contrived, because quite frankly, we'd all been through enough. While there was a great sense of relief, none of us were capable of celebrating yet.

The next morning was Sunday and I arrived bright and early bearing photos (of family and farm animals), Philip's meditation blanket and books and things from home. The hotel room was sterile and dull and I wanted to brighten it up.

A nurse intercepted me on the way to his room. 'We've been waiting for you,' she beamed.

'Why, am I late?' I asked.

'No, but we're getting him up today. There has been great improvement in his strength overnight and the physio thinks he can hold his weight. We wanted you to be here.'

There was much pomp and ceremony as the required medical crew and interested bystanders filed into the room. The changing of the guard at Buckingham Palace couldn't have been more colourful or exciting as 'the day Philip walked'.

The physio, a young woman with a very mature presence, officiated. She issued instructions while the two orderlies followed her every command. Nurses lined the walls and I was given pride of place in front of Philip. With an orderly each side of him for support, he took his first steps. It took all his concentration and determination, and I could see the effort etched as deep lines in his face.

After the initial success, he threw himself into walking with all the determination that he had displayed when throwing himself into flying. Later he confessed that, despite the prediction of months in hospital, he'd decided he was coming home for Christmas and nothing was stopping him.

Seven days after the surgery that, we were told, would at best leave him unable to move from the chest down, he walked out of hospital. The medical staff gave him a hearty farewell. Still nobody could believe the outcome. It was declared a miracle that he had walked again.

Some days later we were discussing this miracle, and I told him the entire conversation that I'd had with the neurosurgeon that morning in the recovery room.

'So,' I challenged, 'what you did was supposed to be impossible, yet your determination overcame all medical opinion.'

'Yes, I guess that is what they call mind over matter,' he pondered.

'What about the cancer? Can you subject that to the same rejection?'

His response chilled me. 'No,' he stated firmly, 'because the doctor didn't tell *me* I'd never walk, she told *you*. A few doctors have told me I'm going to die, and that tape is stuck in my head.'

That conversation marked the beginning of the final twelve months of Philip's life. It was a year so difficult and so painful that I have repeatedly questioned our wisdom in accepting that spinal operation.

Recognise that good people want to help

The tumours were having a field day. The pain levels were exhausting. Philip continued to work hard to walk unassisted and he progressed gradually from a walking frame to a walking stick, but he remained very unsteady on his feet due to some residue spinal damage and the constant pain that he was in. The miracle was amazing but slightly incomplete.

The tumours were also causing night sweats and it was not uncommon for there to be five or six changes of sheets a night. The cancer, in true cancer style, had also starting feeding determinedly on the host, and Philip's weight was dropping rapidly. We were a rather pathetic looking pair. With barely any time for meals, my weight had dropped to under 50 kilos and continued to fall. Neither of us had any clothes that fitted us, nor did we have any time to go shopping.

The medical appointments were frequent and regular, and I was still working long hours in an effort to keep one step ahead of the ever-escalating medical expenses. Fortunately, I had an army of people willing to help. They stepped in at a moment's notice to spend an entire day at the hospital for blood transfusions, and were willing taxis to and from doctor's appointments. My friend Susie set herself up as a co-ordination post and sent out emails to everybody we knew, asking for volunteers to help with running Philip around when I was working.

Susie had willingly agreed to offer this support when I approached her. I felt it would be too hard for people to say no to me and I didn't want people to be put out. By having her approach them instead, it would, I hoped, be easier for them decline if our requests clashed with their plans.

The system worked brilliantly, people put their hands up in droves and Susie meticulously kept details of their daytime and night time contact numbers, regular commitments and possible free times. When we found ourselves stuck (as happened one time when the arranged lift pulled out at the last minute), Susie came to the rescue, and almost immediately had an alternate plan for us.

It seemed like every day there was some appointment or other to attend, more tests, more scans, consultations—the list went on and on. In addition, Philip could no longer be on his own, as he was unable to manage even the simplest of tasks. Again, the army of supporters stepped up to the plate and between us we ensured that Philip always had someone on hand to help him. Wonderful bonus days were when either of my friends Robbyn or Margaret were on 'Philip watch', because then I'd come home to a clean house, the laundry done and a meal ready. On those days, I felt very cared for as well as well supported.

There was no denying that 2006 was a highly challenging year, yet amidst all the angst and pain we worked hard to notice and acknowledge that there were also blessings around us. After all, life is never all bad.

Give (and live) the gift of excitement

Philip's mobility was significantly impaired; however, I agreed without hesitation when one of his daughters rang one day and made what could have been seen as a rather preposterous suggestion.

'Joan, I want to take Dad to the football grand final in Sydney', she stated confidently.

I immediately thought this was a great idea. Philip, I knew, would love it. He was a dedicated sporting addict. He loved cricket, but he was obsessed with rugby league and the Broncos (a team he had followed forever), had made it to the grand final to be played in Sydney.

Of course, this was going to require a logistical plan of such detail and finesse that it would match anything NASA had ever attempted. I knew it was worth it.

I elected not to go. For one reason, I really don't enjoy football (of any code) and knew I'd just be a wet blanket. (I'm banned from friends' grand final events as I talk throughout all the excitement, I've been told.) For another, given that football was a shared passion between Philip and his youngest daughter, it seems fitting that they enjoy this event together.

We launched into planning mode and ensured we had everything in place before we told Philip what was happening. His face lit up. No matter how much pain he was experiencing, I could tell without doubt that when he heard what was being planned (and saw the required tickets as proof) he was resolved to get there and to enjoy it.

One of his brothers lived in Sydney, so the plan naturally incorporated his assistance. Philip boarded the Qantas flight bound for Sydney with a small overnight bag of clothes and a full-sized suitcase of pain management drugs. The tragic comparison provided a very distressing reality check.

True to their word, father and daughter kept me well informed of their travel progress and, knowing that Philip was in caring and careful hands, I resolved to have a few days break. Of course I worried about him, but I also knew that this trip was so very important. I made a commitment to myself to get some downtime, catch up on some sleep and spend time relaxing on the farm. My batteries were well in need of a recharge.

A text message just before kick-off confirmed that they had arrived safely at the grounds and were happily ensconced in their allocated seats. The Broncos got an early lead and Philip couldn't contain himself. His voice when he rang was stronger than I'd heard for months.

'We're in front!' he screamed down the phone about 20 minutes into the first half. I had the game on in the background and looked over towards the television. Sure enough, Darren Lockyer had just converted a try to bring the score to 8 – 4. (They were playing the Melbourne Storm.)

Philip hung up and I went back to my book, already convinced that the trip had been a good plan. The energy in Philip's voice was so much stronger and I could feel his excitement surging its way along the phone lines.

The next call came a few seconds after full time. The noise in the background drowned out any detail, but it was evident from the cheering and whooping that I could hear coming from Philip and the crowd that his beloved team had won.

'Call me later!' I screamed. 'When it's a bit quieter.' The phone went dead.

He rang from the relative calm of his brother's lounge room that night. There was still heaps of whooping and cheering happening, but four people just aren't capable of reproducing the deafening levels of noise that several thousand excited fans are. His voice was strong, and he sounded well and healthy. I was stunned. His articulation was clear and precise and there were no pain-provoked delays between words, no wincing—just clear, loud, excited, wonderful sentences.

Philip returned with almost all of his drugs untouched. He had three full morphine-free days after that football game. The endorphins that his body created during the excitement of tries, conversions and field goals were significantly more effective that any pharmaceuticals had been up until that date or after. Philip found complete temporary pain relief and he relished the next few days as his body soared on the high that the grand final win had created.

I was tempted to phone coach Wayne Bennett and ask if they could please play a grand final every week and win. Endorphin pain relief is instant, completely free and has no side effects (other than lots of laughter and a significant amount of whooping and recounting of moves, plays and player successes).

Don't expect to be ready for everything

The excitement of the grand final over, we were heading towards Christmas, and it was becoming evident that Philip's time with us was reaching the end. Prior to his illness I had been a fence sitter on the subject of euthanasia; however, Philip's cancer swung me well and truly onto the 'pro' team.

In my previous ponderings, I had wondered how you could possibly know that the time when all hope had gone had arrived. That our journey was now barrelling towards an unquestioned destination had become so self-evident that it was undeniable. We had turned a one way corner some time in 2005 and by mid-2006, the word 'hope' had disappeared from our vocabulary.

Philip had had a number of admissions to the palliative care ward and, on each occasion, had signed himself out. He was determined to die at home. I was committed to doing what I could to facilitate that for him. I was also terrified about how we would manage it.

We lived over forty minutes from any hospital, our neighbours were not within calling distance (at least not without a phone) and my family were spread out all over the world. I wanted to honour Philip's wish, but I had no idea how I was going to do it.

With each discharge from the palliative care ward, I got more and more panicky. Our fridge and cupboards were loaded with drugs. Boxes of syringes littered the bench tops of our kitchen. I had learnt how to administer morphine and methadone. I was so far out of my comfort zone that I'd lost sight of any signposts and, despite the truly amazing and dedicated efforts of family and our host of friends, at the end of the day, when everybody went home, I was alone with the demon that had invaded our lives and I was scared.

I knew we were now in countdown and it wasn't long before I was going to have to find a way to manage—or fail Philip by putting him in hospital.

I was still trying to keep my workshops going (purely for financial reasons now) and was in the city running a workshop when we hit the moment that in anybody's terms, was the beginning of the end. Philip had yet another medical appointment that day, and a friend had taken a day off work to transport him.

I had just started the workshop when she rang. In ordinary circumstances I would never answer the phone when at work, but I had explained to the group that we had a family health issue. I had asked them would they mind if I answered if I received a call. They had all resoundingly given their approval. I stepped outside the room to take the call.

'We've got a problem.' The caller's voice was edgy. I could hear her nervousness. 'Philip's had some sort of turn. He doesn't know where he is, and he can't walk properly. I've got him to the oncologist and she is making plans to admit him immediately. She thinks you need to come.' The silence on the other end of the phone confirmed that things were bad.

I felt my own tears follow their now familiar track down my cheeks and looked up to see one of the managers from the organisation where I was working standing before me. He knew Philip well and he knew our story. He had been particularly supportive throughout Philip's illness. Some months earlier when I had arrived for a workshop, he had popped his head in the door as I was setting up. 'How are you?' he asked. 'And before you answer, this is me asking and I want the truth.'

I managed a weak smile. 'I'm crap,' I admitted. 'But I'll pull myself together before the punters arrive.' He came over and gently took out of my hands the pile of workbooks that I was placing on tables. 'Go get a coffee,' he ordered gently, 'I'll do this.'

The support I'd had from this organisation had been outstanding, and if I had to be anywhere working on this day, I was glad it was there.

David saw my tears and his glance went from my face to the phone in my hand. 'I have to go,' I said, my voice breaking. 'It's bad.' He shuffled me over and squeezed onto the chair beside me. Wrapping his arms around me, he just held me into his shoulder for a few seconds and asked, 'How are you getting to the hospital?'

'I'll be fine,' I said. 'Driving and crying are the norm now; but can you explain to the group for me? I don't think I can.'

David immediately went into the room and retrieved my handbag, handed it over to me and asked again, 'Can I get someone to drive you, or call taxi for you and we'll bring your car over later?'

'No, thanks. I'll be fine.'

Months later, after Philip's funeral, I was back in that same training room and one of the participants of the workshop, who had been on the workshop the day I was called to the hospital, came over and asked how I was. When I explained that Philip had passed away, she replied softly, 'I'm so sorry to hear that. It sounded bad that day. David explained it to us. He was crying when he told us—your husband must have been an amazing man.'

I drove to the Prince Charles on automatic pilot and arrived in the now familiar palliative care area. When I arrived, I was quickly taken to a seat. With the matron holding my hand, Philip's position was explained to me. He had gone into kidney failure. We needed to decide what to do.

Not long after, Dr Maree arrived. There was more hand holding as she outlined the options. We could leave things as they were, which would mean he would pass away quite quickly—probably within a couple of days, or we could see about the feasibility of kidney stents. Again, this was not a cure; however, it would provide some relief and it would lengthen his life a bit.

Christmas was looming and I knew Philip loved Christmas. We entered Philip's room as a team. It might well have looked like a posse. I sat on the chair on his left hand side. Dr Maree sat on the bed near me. 'Philip, can you hear me?' she asked. He looked over at her. He was working hard to regain some clarity and, once again, his determination amazed me.

Dr Maree outlined to Philip that there were no more medical options with regard to his cancer. The tumours had now invaded extensive areas of his brain (thus his disorientation) and a massive tumour had blocked his kidney function. We were also aware of tumours in his liver.

'Philip, I need you to know that I've signed a do not resuscitate order. Do you understand what that means?'

Philip nodded almost indiscernibly.

'I've also spoken to a renal specialist at the Royal Brisbane Hospital about possible kidney stents and he is getting back to me. If it is possible to install stents, do you want to undergo that procedure?'

Philip looked over at me and I wanted desperately to say 'no, don't do it'. We were now officially prolonging his agony. This wasn't life saving, this wasn't even life enhancing, this was just cruel in my book. However, despite his difficulty understanding what was happening I still believed he needed to be given a chance to be part of the decision.

The resolve returned momentarily to Philip's eyes, and for the briefest of time he was back. 'I want the stents,' he proclaimed strongly and then instantly relapsed into a foggy state of confusion. The decision, from my point of view, had been made.

Treasure the moments and appreciate the angels

The stents were installed the following day at the Royal Brisbane Hospital and, despite being a difficult and painful procedure, the relief was almost immediate. With the toxins that had been accumulating in his system now released, he showed a marked improvement.

He was transferred back to the Prince Charles and his second daughter moved into the ward with him as his support. This allowed me to continue to look after the farm morning and evening and spend the daytime at the hospital. It also allowed me to make alternate arrangements for all the workshops I had booked for the next few weeks. Despite the ever-arriving bills, it was time for me to stop work for a while.

The following week was a continuous cycle of home, animal feeds, hospital, home, animal feeds and hospital. For the first time in ages, I was also able to get some uninterrupted sleep (with the night sweats and the constant pain, sleep had been something neither of us had really been able to manage for the past couple of years). All talk of dying at home had temporarily ceased, and with his condition slightly improved, we were optimistic that he would see Christmas.

One day I arrived at the hospital to be greeted by Philip surrounded by paperwork. 'What's this?' I asked.

'I'm coming home,' he announced. 'The food here is crap and I want my own bed.'

'Holy shit,' I thought. 'How do we deal with this?'

Several medical staff had tried to talk him out of it, but to no avail. When that didn't work, they worked on me. 'It's impossible,' stated the matron. 'You're too far from medical help and you don't know what you are doing.'

Yes, actually all that was true, but Philip was adamant. In fact, Philip was desperate.

'We're going to give it a try,' I said, feeling like I had just betrayed myself.

Philip wanted to come home with me immediately. I tried to explain to him that we needed to organise equipment. We needed a bed for him—he insisted he could sleep in our bed. We needed a chair for the shower—he wouldn't have a shower, he retorted. Any argument I offered, he saw and raised. Finally, I compromised on the next day. (My preference was for the day after, just to give me some much-needed time to adjust.) I raced home and started trying to get things organised.

A few months earlier, a friend had told me about a Buddhist hospice called Karuna. She'd left me with contact details and suggested that, if we got to that point, I might want to involve them. At this point I wanted to involve anybody, and people who actually knew what they were doing were a huge bonus.

I rang Karuna when I got home and explained our situation. They asked where we lived and I held my breath as the woman I was speaking to went off to check their list to see if they covered our area.

'Yes, we do,' she announced gleefully when she returned to the phone. I couldn't have been happier if she'd just told me I'd won lotto.

They couldn't get a hospital bed or any of the other requirements out to us until the end of the week; however, one of their nurses would visit the next day and assess what we needed and how frequently the service might come out.

The nurse who came to meet me the following day was Kate. She was wearing fantastic shoes. Now I know footwear isn't how you assess people or their medical capability, but her colourful, flat hippie sandals appealed to me greatly. I figured any woman who would wear them could be a friend of mine.

Kate made a list of the items we would need and outlined the services that Karuna could provide. They sounded like angels in comfy shoes to me and my confidence that we could do this started to rise.

After Kate's visit, I headed to the hospital to collect Philip. I was more optimistic now. Kate had helped me find a renewed sense of determination. She had fed my confidence and reassured me that what we wanted to do was possible. She had also promised that Karuna would be there to help us.

The discharge process consisted of me being piled up with more boxes of drugs and syringes and a series of final grim warnings from the matron who reinforced in no uncertain terms that, in her view, I couldn't possibly succeed. She concluded by stating when I'd had enough I should bring him back. I secretly wondered if Philip had paid her to be so negative, because he knew me well enough to know that such statements represented challenges to me and made me more determined than ever to succeed.

Any attempts to find a way to make Philip comfortable in the car completely failed, and despite all my efforts to the contrary, it seemed that the car was determined to find every last pothole on the road.

Philip's children and Kent were all waiting for us when we got home and we set about doing what we could to settle Philip in. It immediately became apparent that we needed the hospital bed as soon as possible, as getting him in and out of our bed was a nightmare. Karuna had promised that everything would arrive in two days, but I was very concerned about how we would manage until then.

The drugs were all piled in the fridge (filling the house fridge and spilling over to the spare fridge in the garage) and a larger section of kitchen bench space was cleared for the additional syringes and swabs. I was less than comfortable with the end result. It made for horrific décor, but I sadly resigned myself to the necessity of it.

As the afternoon wore on, everybody started to make noises about their evening plans and by 5.30 pm, they had mostly all left. Philip's son remained, and it turned out he was my sole evening support that night.

The days got longer and harder. Philip's short periods of mobility decreased each day and his periods of confusion increased. Every so often he would pull a rabbit out of the hat and do something unbelievable. I remember overhearing a conversation between him and a GP on one occasion. Philip was reciting Shakespeare, correctly and in context. The doctor was suitably impressed. 'With all the drugs he has on board, that's amazing. Treasure these moments,' was his farewell comment to me.

With one of the nurses from Karuna arriving each day and the GP in regular attendance, the medical support felt comforting. Philip now had a syringe driver which was automatically administering regular doses of pain relief, and the support team were giving him break-through injections (so when the pain was too much for the syringe driver, we would manually top up with an injection).

The house often felt toxic, as emotions rose and tempers frayed. The only room in the house where I could find any solace was my Reiki treatment room, and I was furious one day when I entered my sacred space to find boxes of hospital supplies tossed carelessly across the floor. I set about moving the boxes and restoring my 'non-dying' room to its peaceful state. I was questioned about what I was doing. How could I explain? My bedroom was a hospital, my kitchen a pharmacy, my bathroom a disability room and my lounge room invariably full of people and completely trashed. All I wanted was one small room that didn't have the symbols of illness and dying draped all over it.

Everybody else got to go home, to return to the peace, quiet and sanctity of a house without cancer, but I was here 24 hours a day, seven days a week. I needed a room I could go to that was free of medical supplies. I needed somewhere where there was order and safety.

This is a really important point and I want to emphasise it. Live-in carers deal with cancer every minute of every day. Everybody else gets to go leave for a period of time. They get to retreat to a bed without illness, to a fridge without drugs, to a house without syringes, to a space without cancer. This restorative opportunity is not afforded to those who live in.

Another time I lost it was when I heard some unfamiliar music being played. It was pleasant enough, so it didn't bother me initially, but when I made enquiries about it, I was told it was music that had been chosen for Philip's funeral. I freaked. Nobody should have to listen to their own funeral music. I couldn't believe that the funeral had already become a primary conversation. 'Maybe,' I remember spitting angrily across the room, 'instead of planning a funeral, somebody could do something useful like wash the bloody sheets?'

We all have our breaking point and I knew I was getting dangerously close to mine. I was done in from the previous four years and I was disintegrating as death inched in ever closer. I know I was hard to be with, and I apologise for that. I was struggling with my roles as doctor, nurse, orderly and cook, when what I really wanted was the return of my roles as partner and friend. These had long since gone by the wayside.

There were no deep moments of contemplation and recounting of memories as there had been with Helen. There were no goodbyes, no hand holding or head stroking. With Philip's care being a full time, round the clock, all-consuming role, there was only time for the essentials and necessities of dying. Living had left our house some time ago. Those who understood this supported me well, and I thank those people from the deep, dark and shattered depths of my soul.

Philip had pretty much taken to his hospital bed (which was now installed in our bedroom) and rarely got up. When he did, it was for very brief periods. Christmas was looming and he seemed aware of that. I was optimistic that we would have him for Christmas. New Year seemed a bit too much to hope for, but then he had constantly defied any predictions made by the medical profession so in reality, so who really knew?

I asked him if there were people he wanted to see and named four. His good friend George (of Ann and George who we'd met in Morocco and who lived in Yorkshire, England), his close buddy and playmate Mike, his dear friend Margaret with whom he worked in Geoff Wilson's office, and a priest.

The first three were obvious choices, but the fourth one surprised me. Previously, before cancer, when we'd discussed our funerals, Philip and I had both expressed a desire for cremation. We wanted a non-religious service at home, followed by transportation to the crematorium and the scattering of our ashes at What If Farm. Two weeks before he died, he announced he had returned to the faith and he wanted a full Catholic funeral with a burial—and he wanted to see a priest. As previously mentioned, Philip had been a monk after leaving school and, as all my Catholic friends assure me, once a Catholic, always a Catholic.

I rang George in England. 'He wants to see you,' I told him. 'We'll pay the airfares. Can you get here?'

There was silence on the other end of the line. George's voice was cracking with emotion when he finally replied, 'I've been wanting to come, but I thought it was family only. Are you sure?'

'I've never been more sure.'

'Give me half an hour.' The phone went silent.

He rang back in the allotted thirty minutes and announced that the earliest flight they could get was Christmas Day, and that they would abandon their own family just after Christmas lunch and see us on Boxing Day.

Then I rang Mike. 'I'm on my way, Joni.' his voice broke as we spoke. He arrived shortly after and lay next to Philip on the bed for ages. I heard them laughing. They were swapping 'boy stories'. Then there were long periods of silence as they said their goodbyes.

Next, I rang Margaret. She and her husband were on the Sunshine Coast holidaying. 'We'll be there tomorrow,' she stated.

Philip was ecstatic when we told him that his friends were on their way. Naturally Margaret and Mike had been regular visitors throughout his illness, but these visits were special ones, because we all knew that these would be the final ones. He asked every few hours whether they were here yet. Finally, we put a countdown chart up on the bedroom window for him so he could see when he could expect everybody.

The priest was a much more difficult proposition. Philip had refused the idea of a service at Sandgate where he had been baptised and taken communion, stating that he was a Samford resident now and that he would be buried from Samford. So I naively headed off to the local Catholic church, expecting to find a man in a long gown, hands pressed together in the prayer position who would gracefully welcome me with 'Bless you, child'. Instead, I found a locked and bolted door and no sign of life.

Plan number two! I contacted a friend, an ex-priest. Surely he would know how I could organise this? He did! He provided me with the number for the diocese and suggested I ask for Father Frank. 'Frank is Philip's type of guy,' he said. 'And you'll like him too'. Well-armed with a name and number, I was now on a mission. After some days of voice messages and return phone calls, I finally got onto the diocese and from there to the man himself (as in Frank, not God).

'I'm in Gympie on holiday' he explained.

'Oh,' said I, somewhat shocked. 'Holidays at this time of the year. Isn't this your busy season?'

Father Frank laughed. 'It's alright. I have a backup.'

On hearing the story, he advised he would come as soon as he could. It could be a couple of days, he said, as he needed to borrow a car. 'Will that be too long?' he asked gently.

'I certainly hope not, Father,' I replied. Once I told Philip that Father Frank was on the way, it was clear that there was no way he would die before the priest got to us. Philip, having returned to all his Catholic 'hell and brimstone' roots, was convinced that if he died without confession he was off to see Satan with no chance of a parole.

Margaret arrived the following morning and spent time with Philip, placing sea shells, sand and ocean water from the Sunshine Coast lovingly by his bedside. He was visibly more relaxed when she left.

When support walks in the door, offer it a seat

Just before Christmas, he went rapidly downhill, and it suddenly appeared that he might not be there for Santa, George or Father Frank. Blood tests were organised, and the results showed that he was heavily anaemic. It was time for another 'do we act or do we let things take its course?' discussion.

I sensed that the GP, like me, thought we were just prolonging the pain now, but we both knew that Philip wanted another Christmas. On that basis, things were organised for a home blood transfusion.

The blood team arrived on a Tuesday. I remember it well. I still call it 'Black Tuesday'.

The arrival of the blood transfusion team was yet another sword into my soul. Emotions are fascinating. I knew, absolutely, that I was about to become a widow. That fact hadn't escaped me by any means, but any action or symbol that confirmed this fact (for example the arrival of the hospital bed, the drugs in the fridge and on this particular day, the arrival of the blood transfusion team) completely unravelled me. I know I wasn't in denial, yet the tangibles of death were too much for me, just too confronting.

I was spinning with confusion. We were playing 'blind man's bluff'. I wasn't blind and this was no bluff, but the awful spinning continued. I wanted everybody to go away, yet I knew I couldn't manage on my own. I'd lost track of what I was most scared of—whether Philip would die that day or whether he wouldn't. Neither situation was manageable for me anymore.

As I stood, shaking with fear, I suddenly became aware of a male voice asking where the power outlets were in the bedroom. I looked up to see a young fellow in jeans holding a plug attached to a blood transfusion machine. The household was crumbling and I had started to seriously wonder what might end first, Philip's life or my sanity.

The transfusion underway, the house continued to reverberate with activity as strangers strode back and forth, checking monitoring machines, drawing up syringes and compiling notes in the notebook we'd installed on the dining room table to record updates and information. (Having a central information register was really helpful. It included all aspects of Philip's care, what he'd eaten that day, what drugs he'd had, and notes between the doctor and the nurses. It was a full account of events all in one spot and meant that we weren't relying on memory and that people didn't have to keep asking me questions. All the answers were already recorded for them to read themselves.)

With a new medical team in situ, I found myself temporarily with nothing to do. That felt strangely uncomfortable and very foreign to me. The house was shrouded in a haze of activity and suddenly out of that haze strode a tall man. His gait was relaxed, and he wore a hybrid look that highlighted both his calm and his concern. He made his way over to me and said, 'Joan?'

I remember nodding, my mind racing to try to remember who he might be. I mentally ticked off all the current attendants at the house. The team seemed present and accounted for. I had no idea who this man could be. On confirmation of my identity he took my hand and started to lead me to the deck. He sat me down in a chair with my back towards the house and moved another chair over in front of me.

'I'm Andrew.' His voice was deep, yet soft. 'I'm a counsellor from Karuna. I can see everything that is happening in the house and I promise to let you know if you are needed. Meanwhile, I want you to just focus on this conversation with me. I'm here to support you.'

The hour with Andrew passed too quickly. For the first time, I felt that I had permission to reveal and release the burning pit of emotions inside me. There was no judgement, no attempt to make things better, no platitudes or suggestions to 'think positive', no competition, just a total, open focus on me. Andrew's ability to be with and manage my pain was extraordinary. Our conversation and Philip's blood transfusion concluded almost simultaneously, and both Philip and I showed evidence of clear improvement as a result of the helpful energy that had been poured into us.

I continued to see Andrew for some time after Philip died. Our sessions moved from soft, gentle talks to the creation of safe spaces for me to healthily connect to and release my anger. This in turn helped facilitate my own healing and return to life.

Endure—and find something to look forward to

Christmas Day finally arrived, and it was a nightmare. Philip, feeling slightly improved after the blood transfusion, managed to get up for a couple of hours, though I could see the effort was too much for him. We were both delighted that we had the whole family, all the children, their partners, my two gorgeous grandsons and an array of family dogs with us for the day.

I had dressed Harry up in reindeer antlers and Rosie was the epitome of sweetness in her angel hat. We swapped presents and enthusiastically wished each other Merry Christmas as we tried to ignore the grim reaper who was hiding just behind the door.

Philip was frail. He was unbelievably skinny and he looked about 150 years old. He was frequently disoriented, and all too often just looked really, really sad. Someone put a Santa hat on him and it felt heartbreaking, almost like we were making a mockery of him. I was torn between allowing the family to express their needs in their way, and feeling like I had to protect Philip from this macabre game of dress up.

His Christmas lunch consisted of a protein shake (which he ignored) and several injections of morphine. He'd made it to Christmas, but was it worth it? His pain levels were now such that even slight contact with his flesh would cause him to flinch in pain. We were all going through the motions and the motions were doing us in.

The effort of the day exhausted Philip, and when he retired back to bed the impact was evident on his face. However, there was another shining motivator on the horizon. Tomorrow was Boxing Day and the George and Ann countdown meter on the window was clearly indicating that there was only one more sleep until they arrived. Philip double-checked with me before he went to sleep. 'Is George coming tomorrow?'

'Yes, he is.'

'Wonderful.' He drifted off to sleep.

Appreciate your friends (and dress appropriately)

The cavalry was coming! I had been doing 24 hour back to back shifts and grabbing snippets of sleep whenever I could. The night sweats continued, and Philip required break-through pain relief sometimes three or four times a night. Every night's sleep for as long I could remember had been disjointed and frequently interrupted. Philip's children had arranged a roster, and most of the time there was at least one of them there. Kent appeared to have moved in and other neighbours and friends would materialise with food, or I would notice them disappearing with bundles of washing. My machine could no longer manage the stream of bed linen that needed to be washed.

To help us manage the multitude of phone calls each day, a friend had been appointed as 'communication central'. She had taken over emails and phone calls, doing everything she could to ensure that people were kept informed. Philip and I both had very public careers and we had established large social networks (individually and together). People were genuinely interested in how he was going and what they could do to help.

I would love to say we were a well-oiled team, but we weren't. Even with all the involvement around us, we were on our knees. Nursing someone is a demanding and exhausting job (and I know many of my friends who are nurses will agree with that statement). Nursing someone you LOVE who is DYING takes exhaustion to a whole other dimension.

We didn't have improvement to look forward to. The best we could hope for was that today was only slightly worse that yesterday. Each morning I would watch the sunrise as I fed animals and face that impossible dilemma. Would today be the day he died? I dreaded that day. Or would today be another day he lived? I dreaded that day, too.

Watching his escalating pain levels was heartbreaking, as was observing his intellectual disorientation. Philip had been an outstandingly intelligent man—scarily intelligent, and the demon was eating away at his brain, leaving just enough cognisance for him to actually realise that it was happening. It, along with his ever-increasing dependence, was horrendously cruel.

That Boxing Day morning, Philip mustered all his effort. He was determined to get up so he could welcome George. He insisted on being helped out of bed at 5.00 am, 'showered' (I could no longer manage actual showering so we had moved to bed baths instead) and dressed. He sat at our outside table watching the gate where the much-awaited car was due to arrive with the much-anticipated, precious cargo sometime around mid-morning.

With no-one there to assist, I was doubling as animal feeder and Philip watcher, and as I raced from paddock to paddock delivering delicious breakfasts to the crew, I could see Philip sitting upright in the chair, supported by cushions and pillows. He didn't take his eyes off the gate for a second.

I returned to the house and made myself a cup of tea and replaced Philip's untouched protein drink (he had ceased taking any solid food some time ago) with a fresh one. I sat with him to share the wait.

'Shouldn't you get dressed?' His gaze didn't leave the gate, but as the only other person present, I was pretty sure he was talking to me.

'I am dressed,' I replied, somewhat confused. Maybe his eyesight was going now as well.

'I mean put something appropriate on. George is coming.'

I looked down at my ensemble. It was hardly appropriate for dinner out or even for a shopping stint, but the faded three-quarter cotton pants, baggy T-shirt and work boots seemed very apt for farm feeding to me. It wasn't right for George, it seemed.

'George is coming to see you, Philip,' I observed as I sat down next to him. 'I don't think he'll mind that I'm in farm clothes.' Again, the gaze didn't leave the gate, but I could see an expression of disapproval on his face. Given the purpose of the visit, I highly suspected that George wouldn't notice what I had on and, if he did, I knew George well enough to know he wouldn't care.

The wait felt interminable. Philip asked every few minutes, 'How long now?' It was like a long car trip with a child, and rather than responding, 'Just around the corner,' I opted for, 'Not too long. Maybe try some of your drink while you wait?' He didn't even sip the drink and he continued to ask for the time updates.

Then I saw his face light up and knew that he had spotted the small sedan as it came around the final bend before our driveway. I could that see he wanted to get up and run to the gate but, even fuelled with his uncontainable excitement, such a journey was impossible for him. I waited with him in case I needed to restrain him. The last thing we needed at that point was a fall.

George was out of the car before it came to a halt, and he sprinted up the driveway. Philip made a move to stand up and I helped him to his feet just as George arrived and wrapped his arms around him. George isn't a big man at all, but he looked massive next to Philip. When George finally disentangled himself from the embrace, Philip looked over at me and smiled, 'George is here,' he said, beaming.

Then he looked back at George. 'I'm sorry Joan is dressed so inappropriately,' he complained. George examined my outfit carefully and replied, 'She never has known how to behave, Philip; we all know that.' Then I was enfolded in George's strong arms and in one hug, I knew that with the team now extended, we were going to make it.

Having now made the trip from the car to the house, Ann immediately busied herself helping Philip back into the chair. She then pried George away from me to make room for her own hug. 'You look like shit,' she stated, her Yorkshire accent sounding like a song from heaven to me. 'When was the last time you ate?' With that, she marched into the kitchen and started to do the dishes.

'What are you doing?' I asked. 'Sit down and have a cup of tea.'

'We're not here to socialise.' Her voice was adamant. 'I'll get these dishes done, then I'm getting you something to eat, and then you can teach us how to do the injections.'

I collapsed into a chair, I thanked every God I've ever heard about and I said the only thing I could think to say at the time. 'There's real orange juice in the fridge.'

For one delicious moment, we were transported back to that roof in Marrakesh when the great director of life was picking the cast for this tragedy was that looming in our future. I watched our amazing friends as they immediately started to busy themselves and I realised that that cosmic director had picked very, very well indeed.

Find your rhythm

Ann took over running the household, and it was heaven. The delicious aromas of home-cooked meals filled every room and chaos was magically transformed into order. George took over all Philip's bathing and dressing needs and the rest of us responded to medication requirements and trying to entice Philip to try some of the protein drink. We were cooking with gas again. With the calls intercepted, the phone was much quieter and we were all able to get snippets of down time to relax.

Ann's insistence that I eat extended to following me around the house with a bowl of pasta, shoving spoonfuls into my mouth whenever I opened it to protest. My weight had hit an all-time low of 47 kilos, so I understood her obsession with my diet, but food was starting to sit heavy in my stomach. My digestive system was lodging some painful and difficult objections.

One night Ann helped me to do the feeds. As I was mindlessly piling hay into the donkey hayfeeder, her question brought me back to the moment with a jolt. 'Is this donkey normally lame?' I looked over and there was Eeyore on three legs.

'Shit. No, he isn't,' I exclaimed, defeat ringing out through my words. Somehow, after all the hospitals, tests, operations, doctor's appointments, treatment visits, blood transfusions, you name it, with all that we'd been living with for the past four and a half years, somehow, Eeyore on three legs just felt like the final straw. I realised with despair that I had no idea what to do.

Ann understood my confused shoulder shrug immediately. 'We'll sort it,' she said, approaching the three-legged donkey in a bid to try to assess the problem. Eeyore was having none of it. He was sore and he wasn't going to be handled and for a boy on three-quarter steam, he moved quickly.

'Let's leave him tonight,' she suggested, closing the gate that allowed them access to the big paddock. 'They can stay in here so we can keep an eye on him. If he's no better in the morning, I'll organise a vet. He'll be fine. You don't need to worry about this one.' As soon as we vacated the hay feeder, Eeyore made his way over, shoving Jesus out of the way, but all the time ensuring he kept a watchful wary eye on us in case we decided to try to look at that hoof again.

Ann laid her arm across my shoulders as we walked back to the house. 'Nobody is going to think less of you if you send him to hospital,' she said gently.

'I know they won't,' I replied. 'But I will feel that I've let him down.' We both knew we weren't talking about the donkey.

Be true to your beliefs and allow
others to be true to theirs

Eeyore was still hobbling the next morning and I returned from the morning feed run feeling deflated.

'He's not really that much worse.' Ann was waiting for me with a cup of tea when I got back to the house. 'I popped down earlier to check him. He still won't let me lift his foot, though. What time does your vet open? George and I will sort the donkey.'

I sighed the umpteenth sigh of relief since Ann and George had arrived less than forty-eight hours earlier. Dying definitely requires a team effort, and our team had been dedicated and willing, but just too light on the ground. With two more positions filled, it now felt like we had sufficient bases covered.

It was not even 5.00 am and the house was already a hive of activity. Despite his obvious disorientation, this morning Philip was making it clear that he wanted to get out of bed and to be helped to get dressed. He was indicating which clothes he wanted, and George was patiently and carefully attending to his needs. The reason for the excitement was that Father Frank was coming today, and even with his drug-fuzzed brain, Philip had remembered his appointment with the priest.

With Philip showered (properly this morning—George stripped both of them off and they showered together) and dressed, he demanded to be positioned in the lounge chair. He proceeded to wait, impatiently, for his chosen representative of God.

'Father Frank said he'll be here about 9.00,' I advised and placed a large digital clock next to him showing the time to be 6.45 am. 'You've got some time to wait. Are you sure you don't want to lie down?'

Philip looked at me as though I'd just suggested he cut off both his big toes. He determinedly pushed himself further into the chair. We weren't getting him out of that waiting position without a fight; that much was very clear.

Ann rang the vet when they opened at 7.30 am and was cheerily advised that someone would be out to attend to Eeyore—also at 9.00. It seemed we had a clash of the saviours.

One thing I was determined to do was to continue to treat Philip like the intelligent man he was. So often, particularly in situations where there is brain damage or memory loss, patients get excluded or interacted with as if they are mindless babies. As with the Shakespeare example mentioned earlier, every so often snippets of the old Philip returned, and when they did, I wanted to make them welcome. Accordingly, I made an effort to continue to interact with Philip as I always had. That included our propensity for jokes and somewhat silly observations.

I took him another protein drink. (Occasionally we managed to get a few sips into him so I had resolved to keep trying.) I perched on the arm of the chair next to him as I held the glass out towards him. 'Eeyore's lame,' I advised casually. 'The vet's on the way, and should arrive about the same time as Father

Frank. I hope we don't mix them up. You might end up with a
foot examination.'

'Why would Father Frank want to look at my feet?' he enquired,
his face revealing his complete confusion. Complete sentences
were sporadic now, and according to the GP a complete miracle,
so I relished the response, even though he couldn't connect to
the joke.

The vet and the priest were old friends and greeted each
other warmly. Ann and George had successfully contained
both donkeys in the barn and were on hand to assist with the
examination. Highly experienced horse people, they were,
without doubt, the best people for the donkey-wrangling job
(remembering that my two gorgeous asses were still essentially
wild boys).

Father Frank swept into the house with the air of a man
accustomed to death and dying. If there truly is a God, then
Frank had been hand chosen. For me, he epitomised the love
and caring that, I believe, is the fundamental message of all
religions. He glanced around the house and his eyes rested
on the Buddha statues and prayer flags. 'You're not Catholic I
assume, Joan.' His voice held a lilt of unconditional caring, and
in his eyes I saw a welcome so loving that I was drawn totally
into his gaze.

'No, Father', I replied.

'But you have strong beliefs, and it's love that counts, Joan.
There could be no greater love than what you are doing now. I
will ensure you are involved in Philip's ceremony. God doesn't
differentiate; he teaches us inclusion.' I silently sent thanks to

my ex-priest friend, Laurie for suggesting Frank. I knew the instant I met him that we had the right person for all of us.

Father Frank spent the next two hours with Philip and Philip was noticeably less agitated when the priest left.

'I've given him all the sacraments, I've re-baptised him, he has taken communion, received the last rights and re-taken his monk's vows,' he outlined for me.

I was a bit dumbfounded, and the only thing I could think of to say was, 'Sounds like a busy morning, Father.'

Father Frank smiled and spent the next few minutes connecting with each person present, checking in, even asking about the donkey (who had undergone a minor procedure on his hoof and been prescribed painkillers—as if we didn't have enough painkillers in the house already).

Advising he would be back the following day, he asked that we contact him when Philip passed, irrespective of what time it was. Had I have been in the market for a religion, Father Frank would have been my choice.

That week, as Christmas made way for New Year, has now become just a 'blob' in my memory. The days have merged, and while there is much that remains very clear, the sequence and dates of some of the events have blurred to produce an activity-filled heartbreaking collage rather than a series of static pictures.

After that initial visit by Father Frank, Philip became progressively more disorientated. As his pain levels ascended to new, unbelievable heights, the drug dosage in the syringe driver was stepped up.

The Karuna nurses came each day, bringing with them a comforting blanket of calm to our house. Nothing was too much trouble; everybody was to be cared for. Their service extended way beyond the patient. They made 'holistic' into an art form. In addition to the nurses, one of the Buddhist nuns came to spend time with me, and Andrew continued to make regular visits to support me. That first day when Kate arrived, she had explained that Karuna don't offer 'care'; they offer you a family in your time of most need. I continue to feel part of the Karuna family now, some eight years down the track.

Father Frank also visited every day, and I enjoyed witnessing his interactions with Philip, the household and the nurses. The day of the nun's visit was a particular highlight for me as I watched Father Frank offer blessings and prayers amidst the serene glow of the Buddhist saffron. It was an ecumenical scene worthy of photographic honouring. You'll be surprised to know that I had no idea where either my phone or my camera were, and somehow, rushing round saying 'hold that pose!' seemed a bit inappropriate.

The days felt long and arduous, and the nights were sleepless and lonely. I was counting down the hours to widowhood and watching in horror as the cancer consumed Philip. With the role of pseudo medico overriding my role as partner or friend, I compared the experience of supporting Helen and supporting Philip, and resolved to instruct my children that they were never to nurse me in this way.

The hospital, while sterile and clinical, provides the space for the family to remain just that. The home environment demands that you abandon your family roles in favour of jobs more medically necessary and demanding. The hospital felt like a luxury to me. My home had transitioned from being a dance floor to a battlefield.

But even the most hardened of soldiers will offer a raft of glorious stories to complement their war wounds and our final days with Philip offered many wonderful moments. I remember the house being filled with the sound of George's singing as he shared the double shower in our en-suite with Philip. He bathed Philip lovingly, loudly singing 'shower' songs to him as he gently cleaned and soothed his emaciated body.

I also recall Ann's storytelling as she reminisced with Philip— colourful stories of camel riding in Morocco and funny snippets of adventures in exotic Kasbahs. Evenings were spent as the community we'd become, gathered around the bedside. Kent's guitar guided us all in special songs that Philip had always enjoyed.

Cancer is horrific, there is no other word for it, but in those final moments, we finally found a sacred, gentle rhythm that would allow us to see the process through.

Say goodbye with love and peace

It was New Year's Eve and we were not planning a party. Philip's children had all taken the night off and headed to the Gold Coast to welcome 2007 with friends and fun. Ann cooked dinner. My body had some time back taken to completely rejecting food, though I was still unable to convince Ann of that. I took the bowl thrust resolutely into my hands and wandered down to the bedroom. 'I'll eat with Philip,' I said and refused all offers of company. Of course the others all understood perfectly, and set up their meal on the deck to take dinner under the stars.

Philip was peaceful when I entered the room, though his body flinched when I settled onto our queen bed, which was pushed up against his hospital bed. Harry came in with me and gently jumped up beside me. His agility and ability to land on the bed without moving it amazed me and I watched tearfully as he sidled up to his master to lie beside him. His loving Border Collie body stretched along Philip's now gaunt, almost unrecognisable frame and he moved Philip's hand gently with his nose. He carefully positioned his soft, furry head directly underneath Philip's palm. With a gentle sigh, he settled himself down. Loyal to the last breath, Harry was to maintain that position for more than 48 hours.

I rearranged my pillows so I could prop myself up, adopting a half reclining position to lay on my left side, my gaze then able to devote itself to Philip. I mindlessly moved the food around the bowl. His breathing was shallow but not laboured, and when I stroked his hand, I noticed his eyelids flicker.

'The year is about to end,' I whispered to him. Harry suddenly shuffled, moving his head slightly and I noticed that he too had positioned himself so he could better see Philip. As we both watched, a soft light gathered around Philip's body. The light lifted slowly and gradually formed a hovering shape beside the bed. The shape was clearly Philip. A strong, vibrant, healthy Philip. Harry and I were both motionless as we witnessed this now clear image of the man Philip had been move his hands gently across the 'vehicle' he was leaving.

He 'touched' each part of himself, stroking his weak, spindly legs, his skeletal torso, and his withered arms. The 'soul hands', rested on their own physical face and head and then the spirit head lifted, and with peaceful, painless eyes, the energy that was Philip gazed first at Harry and then at me.

Our eyes locked for some seconds; a tranquil, loving smile lit up his face. It was the most serene moment I have ever experienced. His smile was filled with love, it spoke of freedom, oozed comfort, reassured me that he was going to a safe place, and that he was finally being released from the painful hell he had been living. I blew him a kiss and watched tearfully as the 'soul self' gently faded and disappeared.

The body on the bed beside me kept breathing, but Harry and I both knew that Philip had gone. It was just as a driver might step out of a car and leave the engine running. It was to be another fifty-one hours before the vehicle ran out of petrol and finally stopped.

Philip's official date of death is 2 January 2007, but Harry and I both know that he left us at 7.05 pm on 31 December 2006. We like to think he had a party to go to in heaven.

Cherish the memories and look after koalas

There is a post script to the Kelvin story and it occurred on 11 May 2007. It was a few months after Philip's passing and the fifth anniversary of us moving into the house. I had completed my usual evening feeds, though was feeling somewhat heavy of heart. The day held so many wonderful memories and also a great deal of sadness, and I completed the evening feed slowly, stopping for extra hugs with each of the animals. It was like they knew that it was a special day. They all spent time with me—the donkeys were happy to leave their feed buckets and come over for cuddles and the alpacas nuzzled at my hair as I sat in the barn with them.

I finally strolled back up to the house, got myself a meal and poured a glass of wine. I sat out on the deck where we had, just a few years before, made our commitment to each other and raised my glass towards the heavens. 'I hope you're ok up there,' I said, 'and I hope that you are marking this day as well.'

The meal and my solo anniversary celebration complete, I headed back into the house. Harry and Rosie started running from one end of the house to the other, tails aloft in excitement, barking like crazy. Their main focus was on the back door. Suspecting the presence of some wildlife (we had a resident snake called Surprise at the time—so named because he loved popping up where you least expected him), I settled the dogs, instructed them to stay inside and went out to investigate what might be getting them so worked up.

Outside the alpaca barn was a large log. It made a perfect 'sitting and being' place, and I would often position myself there to alpaca-gaze after I'd finished the morning feed. I loved watching them idly chewing their hay and their rhythmic crunch, crunch, crunch was incredibly soothing.

Despite the dim light of early evening, I immediately spotted the source of the dogs' interest. There, sitting on my relaxation log, was Kelvin. He was facing into the alpaca barn, his back towards where I was standing at the back door. He sat perfectly still, watching the alpacas eating in the much the same way that I had sat only that morning.

'Oh no,' I thought to myself, 'Kelvin's injured.' This behaviour from a koala is unheard of. To be sitting so close to the ground leaves them very vulnerable. (They prefer the safety of trees, for obvious reasons.) I returned to the house to get a torch and decided I would try to creep up to him to see if I could establish how badly hurt he was. I also grabbed my phone (which had the number for the wildlife rescue group programmed into it).

As I approached the log, Kelvin didn't move except to turn his head towards me as I got close. He stared intently at me and, aware that the torch light would be disturbing for him, I cast it downwards. This allowed enough light to see without dazzling him too much. Kelvin sat there while I completely circled him. There was no evidence of injury and he appeared alert and happy.

My instinct told me that he was fine; it also told me it was ok to spend some time with him. I sat on the log next to him. The sensor lights in the barn came on, so I extinguished the torch. We sat there together for about 15 minutes, watching the alpacas. Every so often Kelvin would turn his head to look at me.

He was close enough for me to touch him, but I resisted the urge, remembering that whatever was motivating him to sit there, he was still a wild animal (with very long claws).

Eventually, Kelvin turned, met my gaze again, scrambled down from the log and walked slowly past me. He stopped right next to my leg and looked deeply into my eyes. Tears dropped slowly from my cheeks, and for one insane moment I thought he was going to reach up and wipe them away. Instead, he took his leave, very, very slowly, stopping every few yards to turn back and look at me. I watched him disappear into the darkness and then sat alone for what felt like hours.

I rang a friend, a vet nurse with a special interest in wildlife, and told her what had just happened.

'Koalas don't do that!' she exclaimed.

'But it did, I assure you,' I responded.

'Yes and we both know that Kelvin wasn't alone. Philip was always one to find a way. When you see that koala again, tell him I like his style.'

Philip in London - pre cancer.

Kelvin Koala

Philip with Harry and Rosie

The 'Alpaca Shack' construction crew - Mike, Adrian, Harry, Rosie and Philip

Philip preparing to go flying - a dream he had
held all his life and successfully fulfilled.

New hats - lovingly handcrafted presents
when Philip started Chemotherapy

Jesus and Eeyore at What If Farm (with
Duncan and Renoir in the background)

Philip at Stradbroke Island walking with Harry and Rosie

Grand Final Fever - Sydney 2006

Final Days - Philip and I with Ann December 2006

Mischief and I at What If Farm

What If - we found the courage to have strength in adversity,
hope in fearful situations, adventure in uncertainty and joy
in friendships - then we will surely have lived a dream.

A summary of ideas that might help

(please note: the following are suggestions only. Naturally the best ideas are the ones you feel most comfortable with.)

Picking a doctor

This is a very personal decision and the following is offered as some food for thought only. Please remember the 'best' doctor is the suitably qualified doctor you feel most comfortable with.

- There is no 'right' or 'wrong' doctor, though as our story suggests, there are incompetent doctors out there (as with any profession). If in doubt, seek another doctor. This is too big a situation to be left to chance in my opinion.

- If you aren't happy with the process and/or the interactions you are having with your doctor, move on to another doctor. Contrary to some perceptions the doctor is not 'God'. Doctors are fallible, normal human beings with personalities and communication preferences. When a doctor isn't for you, it doesn't mean anybody is 'wrong' or 'bad'. It just means that a better fit may be required.

- Knowing what you need from a doctor in terms of interactions is really helpful. As our story suggests, Philip and I had very different needs. Philip was more comfortable with a direct style, whereas my personality type prefers more connection and interaction. Neither approach is 'better', but being aware of what's important to you is helpful when selecting doctors to work with.

It was very important to Philip and I to find and work with doctors who were prepared to answer questions, review and discuss research undertaken by us or people around us and who were able to offer the time for discussion to support clarity and our understanding.

I remember arriving at Dr Maree's (oncologist) office one day with 90 handwritten pages of research into 'alternate/natural' treatments for prostate cancer. Maree happily took the aforementioned pages and on our next visit had prepared her own list of questions for the author of the document (a highly educated and well-informed friend of ours). 'He has raised some interesting points, Philip,' she announced. 'And I would really appreciate some further information about these aspects.' Maree's support of our need for more information and to be present at the cutting edge of research was both helpful and important to us. This doesn't mean it's the 'right' approach, but it worked for us.

- Similarly, it helps to align with a doctor who is on the same page as you in relation to alternate or complementary approaches. If you decide to pursue these options as well as allopathic pathways, it can be distressing if you aren't supported by your medical team.
- Be prepared to question and clarify. The more you understand what is happening, the better placed you are to manage things and make decisions. There is a fine line between pessimism and reality sometimes.

My view is that if we don't know the worst case scenario, then we aren't in an informed position to develop a strategy to manage it or anything else that might happen. As I mentioned in the story a couple of times, I believe it is better to have a strategy you don't need than need a strategy you don't have. I have found that to be a very helpful mantra for life.

Walking the balance between 'expecting the worse' and 'preparing for the worse' requires delicate footwork, but I found being prepared for the worst can be very helpful in terms of providing a solid fall-back position. Knowing you have that fall-back position can offer some peace of mind. Just because you have a disaster plan doesn't mean the disaster will automatically happen. We all have fire evacuation plans and that certainly doesn't guarantee a fire but it's a great thing to have if there is one.

- Ultimately though, remember that your health is your business, so whatever choices you make around doctors and treatments, be prepared to be involved and don't be afraid to 'doctor shop'. Giving some thought to what you want in your relationship with your doctor before you go shopping can be useful. Know what you need and find a doctor/s who will work 'with you' in the style that is most helpful for you.

Allopathic or complementary approaches?

The answer to this question can only considered in the context of what is actually happening, what treatment avenues are available, the potential outcomes and impacts of all options on the table and your own personal views and belief systems.

- We were scorned by some for not going the surgical route. Surgery is a valid option for prostate cancer when the cancer is contained to the prostate. In Philip's case, we knew early that this wasn't the case and I still stand behind our decision not to go with the knife. However, the advice of Dr Ian Gawler also rings in my ears and I am in agreement with him around the sensibility of taking, with both hands, all options that might be helpful.

- Second, third and even fourth opinions can help to clarify, but ultimately it is your decision which route to take. Keep your ears and eyes open for any new information and delegate research roles to others.

In these wonderful times of information accessibility, the potential for research is endless. Gathering together a research team can help cut to the chase. When people ask 'what can we do?' (and they will) one option is to ask them to gather and summarise information for you. In hindsight, I've realised that we could have identified questions and assigned them to people to research answers and options. There is such a lot of material out there; having some of it 'vetted' (that is, having someone go through articles and books and identify ones that have information about specific types of cancer or particular drugs) would have been really helpful for us and may be for others.

Joan Wilson-Jones

Ideas for the carer

The caring role is a significantly more difficult role than I had anticipated. Maybe I was just a little naïve, but as Philip's illness progressed I found myself constantly self-questioning and self-doubting. This was, by far, the toughest 'gig' I have ever undertaken. I say this not to scare you but to inform you. So, having said that, here are some ideas on how to make it more bearable.

- Set up a support group for you, the carer. This is essential, and the earlier one is set up the better. Some people will think they should only be doing things for the patient directly, but your real friends will realise that by helping you, they are also helping the patient.
- Make a list of food you and other family members enjoy. Ideally, make up some folders of your favourite recipes, which could be offered to people who want to get meals for you. As we got further and further down the path of treatment, disappointments, hospital schedules and sleepless nights, one of the things I was often asked was 'do you want me to cook you a meal?' The idea sounded wonderful, but asked 'what do you want?' I was often too tired and too overwhelmed to be able to come up with an answer (and as a committed 'foodie', I am ordinarily driven by food).
- It also helps to ensure your food preferences are clear. In the absence of any direction from me, well-meaning people arrived with casseroles. This was a wonderful gift, but having been a vegetarian for years, the aromatic beef stew wasn't really high on my list of favourites. (See another note on this in suggestions for carers of carers below.)

- Set up a 'central record'. My friend Sue-Ellen instigated this for us. She delivered a suitably labelled notebook with instructions to all members of the household to note in it anything relating to Philip (what food he'd taken, what drugs he'd been given—any information at all). The Karuna nurses and our GP quickly got on board as well and used the notebook every day to leave instructions, information or a summary of what they had done. This dramatically reduced the constant questions directed at me. On arrival, every support team member (medical or non-medical) would start their visit with a scan of the book. It meant everybody was up to date with information and nobody had to keep repeating the same thing over and over again.

- Keep your interests going! This isn't selfish, it's important. I have a favourite quote from Eleanor Brown— *Self-care is not selfish. You cannot serve from an empty vessel.* This is advice I now provide regularly to new parents as well as all other carers. We are not doing anybody any favours if we put ourselves so much at the end of the line that we burn ourselves out. If people ask what they can do, one answer is to take time to be with the patient for short periods of time so as to enable the carer to have some time to relax. (You don't even have to leave the house. You can curl up with a book, knowing that there is somebody there to manage things if needed.)

- Be aware of your own beliefs and preferences, but be prepared for the person you are supporting to make their own decisions. I remember a conversation with my friend Helen during her treatment for breast cancer. She had looked over at me on this particular day and said, 'you know, sometimes I really think this must be harder for you than me'.

I was pretty surprised. 'Don't be silly', I retorted, 'you're living with this bloody monster, I'm just a spectator'.

'Except that I get to make decisions that feel right for me. I know you well enough to know that you probably would make other decisions if it were you, yet your role is to support me anyway.'

As carers, our role is to support the person 'anyway', and I found this was easier when I was clear about my own position. Then I could separate what I believed or was aligned to from what was happening. None of us are completely 'right' and there is rarely a universal 'better' way. When we can sit comfortably with our own ideas in the midst of decisions that are contrary to them then we can better find some peace.

- If decisions made by the patient challenge you too much, look for ways to marry your beliefs with their responses. Philip's initial foray into heavy drinking (when treatment started) was understandable; however, it provoked all sorts of distress in me. Finally I resolved to accept his choices around alcohol (which he managed better as his initial shock receded) and reduced some of my fears by suggesting organic wines. It was a small step, but it helped pacify me a little and allowed me to manage my own panic a bit better.
- Give people permission! Let people know what it's okay or not okay to do for you or in your home. In the later stages of Philip's illness when life felt really

chaotic, it was really helpful when my friend Sue-Ellen arrived with signs and notes. She pasted a list inside the pantry noting the regular food items that we used and suggested that visitors might check supplies and, if we were low, pick up items for us. She noted instructions for the washing machine and invited people to feel free to throw a load through during their visit.

The appearance of invitations, suggestions and signs was really helpful as people were less inclined to feel uncomfortable about getting in and doing things. It also meant they knew that what they were doing was useful and appreciated and it really took the pressure off me, because I didn't have to come up with ideas when asked 'what do you need?'

- Set up a tea and coffee station in the kitchen. This means that visitors can not only get themselves a drink, but are also able to offer you one as well (a list of how household members prefer their tea or coffee is also helpful).
- If you are in a financial position to do so, pay for help in the house. I know this isn't an option for everybody, so I've included another approach in the list for 'carers of carers' below. As illness progresses, caring becomes more than a full time role. There is no time or energy for housework or garden maintenance, yet neither disappears and both need to be attended to.

I recall one afternoon stepping outside the house to be greeted by a group of neighbours. 'We're here for training!' they announced.

'That's great because I'm a trainer,' I replied. 'What would you like training in?'

'The farm schedule, who gets fed what, where the food is, where the house keys are, what needs to be done—everything!' they announced. 'If you get caught up at the hospital, we're here to step in and do what needs to be done'.

One time when I did need to call on them for help, it was wonderful to arrive home late, tired and distressed, to find all the animals fed and tucked up for the night, the washing in and folded and a home-cooked meal waiting for me on the kitchen bench.

If you have pets, it is essential to have an emergency care strategy ready for them just in case you are delayed. They can't feed themselves..

- Have people to talk to. Again, if possible, engage professional help. It's is not a sign of weakness — it is an investment in self-care. It can be extraordinarily helpful (for both you and the patient) for you to have a neutral, professional set of ears to help you through your own thoughts, fears and discussions. We don't need to wait until we collapse to engage professional support. I'm a strong believer in preventative medicine at all levels.
- If paying for counselling sessions is out of your budget, look at the services of local hospice providers. My interactions with the counsellor at Karuna (the palliative care organisation who helped us) were invaluable, and they were free. Plus, as discussed in the

story, the counsellor came to me when it was impossible for me to be anywhere but with Philip.

- Have cancer-free time. Philip and I made times where we'd put cancer outside for a while. This wasn't about ignoring it, any more than putting the kids with a baby sitter while you have a night out is about forgetting about the children or being in denial about being a parent. It gives you a break. 'Cancer-free times' need to be discussed and decided on together so as to avoid the 'I don't want to talk about it' syndrome that can feel dismissive if the other person isn't part of the strategy.

- Keep a store of your favourite movies on DVD, your favourite music on your iPod or CD and your favourite books on the book shelf or electronic reader. Allow yourself the space to enjoy some time with them. I found that even just a few minutes lost in a book or surrounded by music could be really restorative, but it's hard to put this into place if, when you need it, you have to run to the shop to get the supplies! Your favourite bubble bath waiting in the cupboard might entice you to use it, whereas the thought of going to the shop to get some just makes the whole idea seem impossible.

- One thing I wished we had done was to set visiting and, more especially, 'no visiting' times. Let people know what times they are welcome and when you need to be left alone and given space. It's clearer for them and means your 'down time' won't be suddenly (and lovingly) snatched away by well-meaning visitors. Give yourself permission to hang (either literally or metaphorically) a 'do not disturb' sign on the door.

- Allow yourself to decide who visits. Illness and impending death can spark a need in others to resolve their own past or to be seen as being there. Heartfelt goodbyes are essential. Ex-spouses trying to deal with their own guilt can just be in the way. Sometimes the greatest courage we can show is being able to say 'this isn't the time'.

Ideas for carers of carers—useful and practical things you can do to help

Carers need to be cared for. It is essential if they are going to get through this situation with their health and wellbeing intact. I had amazing support and care and I can't thank the people around me enough.

- Be there for the carer! Devote time and space to the person who is doing the caring. As discussed in the story, being a carer can leave you feeling invisible. Often, without thinking, people would start conversations with me by asking about Philip. There were many conversations where I wasn't asked at all how I was doing.

  Nobody makes us invisible on purpose, and it's easy to slip into a concern about the patient and overlook the carer. This is not an 'instead of' suggestion, it's an 'as well as'. Make a point of asking the carer how they are doing and take time to wait for their answer— especially as the illness progresses. The longer the carer role goes on and the more intense it becomes the greater the risk to the carer.

  I heard a few stories of carers dying before the person they were caring for and, to be honest, there were times towards the end of Philip's illness when I seriously wondered which one of us his cancer would take first. It meant heaps to me when friends made a point of checking in on me specifically. Naturally, this only feels good if it is genuine, and sometimes we need to remind ourselves to do it.

- To help with identification of suitable meals, if you are part of the family or a friend of the carer, 'interview' the carer to determine favourite foods or identify recipes. Maybe you could then compile a number of folders ready for the carer to offer to people who want to help with meals.

- Being close to the carer and the person they are caring for is often distressing for people. I think it's important to express feelings and I think it would be odd if people visited the home of a dying person and didn't get distressed. Remember, however that you can go home and fall apart. You are not helping the patient or the carer if they end up having to care for you as well. Again, this is a fine line, as only a robot would show no emotion, but please be mindful of whose needs are being looked after when you are with the carer.

- It's easy to fall into the trap of trying to relate by competing. I'm not suggesting that you can't share your challenges with carers (it would be a one sided relationship if we did that), but be mindful of where the person is. Sometimes, it's helpful if the carer can have the floor for a while.

Just a few days before Philip's last Christmas I remember talking to someone who, on hearing that things were difficult and very uncertain (as in we didn't know if he would survive to see Christmas) exclaimed that they knew exactly how I felt because they were uncertain about their plans for Christmas as well. They weren't meaning to be insensitive. They were probably just making conversation. As I said in the book, sometimes silence (and listening) is the best option.

- Set up a register of people who can help. In it, note possible availability, best contact numbers etc. My friend Susie did this for us and it was fantastic. If ever I needed some help getting Philip to doctor's appointment or, in one instance, transporting him and staying with him for a blood transfusion, Susie would send out messages and people would respond straight away. It meant we always had plans in place for whatever needed to happen.
- Install a 'communication central'. As the illness progressed I found this to be invaluable. All we, the support team, had to do, was make a daily call to update the 'communication central' person and then they would take all the phone calls and manage all the emails. It meant that people were kept up to date and our home phone was able to enjoy some blissfully long silent periods. (Phones and emails can be forwarded to communication central as well.)
- I remember friends arriving one day with all manner of cleaning products and devices and spending the day scrubbing and vacuuming. This was before 'marvellous Marg' joined our team, and I had been desperately trying to keep up with the housework as well as everything else.

As I have mentioned above, not everybody is in a financial position to pay for house cleaning. Having friends pitch in and help can be particularly useful in these instances. If friends are in a financial position to kick in some funds, then paying for cleaning services would be a much-appreciated gift.

- Similarly, lawns keep growing, as do weeds and gardens. A group of Philip's work mates would descend with mowers, slashers and willing hands every couple of months and do a blitz on our property. It was fantastic. I did my best to keep the maintenance going, but realistically, it was beyond me. The 'garden group' would spend the entire morning working.

  They also brought lunch and, if he felt well enough, would spend time with Philip out on the deck after the work was finished. He looked forward to these visits immensely. Philip's friend Margaret organised the group and would contact me beforehand. Together, we'd draw up a list of any specific things to be done, which Margaret added to her 'ongoing general maintenance' list. On arrival, the team were well-organised and totally independent. If you are looking for something to do to help somebody close to you, then maybe getting a group of happy garden elves together could be just the thing.

- If you are comfortable doing so, offer to spend some time with the person being cared for and provide the carer with some respite. On a couple of occasions friends arrived in pairs, one to stay with Philip and the other to whisk me away for a quick coffee and some fresh air.

- Be aware of the carer's time limitations when organising gifts or helpful gestures. For my 50th birthday, I received a voucher for a therapeutic massage. I can't tell you how helpful it would have been if only *I could have gotten there to enjoy it*. The opportunity to drive to the other side of Brisbane and lay on a massage table for an hour didn't present itself until after Philip died, by which time the therapy centre concerned were adamant that the expiry date had passed and it wouldn't be honoured. (They held firm to this despite my explanations for not being able to get there earlier.)

If you do want to provide the carer with a voucher for some pampering, make sure the supplier is compassionate enough to honour it after the use by date if necessary. Another idea might be to organise a home massage or healing process and to be there to provide some support for the patient so that the carer can have a blissfully indulgent hour or so for themselves. I remember my friend Laurie arriving one day and just demanding that I get on my own massage table (I use it for Reiki sessions). An hour with Laurie and his magic Kinesiology hands, and I felt like I'd had a week at the beach (no joke). Don't be limited to massage. If the carer's belief systems align, look at other healing/relaxing therapies as well (and if they can be offered at home, so much the better).

Here are some seemingly little things that meant a lot to me:

- coming home from hospital late after a very difficult night and seeing the flashing red light on the phone indicating there was a message. It was so comforting to hear my friend Terri's voice. 'I know you're at the hospital and feel free to ring me back if you need to talk, and it doesn't matter what time it is. I just wanted to make sure you heard my voice when you got home and knew I was thinking of you'. It was a simple act that warmed my heart big time

- another phone call, this time from my friend Margaret. 'Joni, I don't know what to do or what to say so I'm ringing to say I don't know what to do or what to say and if there is anything I can do or say please tell me. Meanwhile, I love you'. Perfect, Margaret—thank you

- meeting up with a friend in Sydney one time when I was there for work. She greeted me with 'I'm going to ask about Philip later, but I want us to spend the first ten minutes talking about you and how you are'. What a great 'invisibility deterrent' that was

- people kidnapping the washing and bringing it back washed, dried, folded and ready to put away

- the shopping elves who arrived with groceries and loaded the pantry

- the cooking elves who either dropped meals over or produced wonderful tasty fair in my kitchen.

To finish, here are some potential traps and some ideas for how to avoid/redeem them

- Watch what you say. I talked about the positive thinking movement in the story. It was a difficult part to write as it's a delicate subject and we are all different in how we respond to it. I found comments like 'think positive and it'll all be fine,' to be very dismissive, but nobody wants to dwell on doom and gloom either. Maybe try, 'that sounds awful! What could I do to offer you help and support?' Acknowledging the difficulty and gently supporting the person to some 'helpful' (a term I much prefer to 'positive') thinking might be a useful approach.

- Be prepared to take a step back and retrieve the situation. I remember being in North Queensland working with Sue-Ellen when we received some horrific test results. I sank (physically and emotionally) and Sue-Ellen, seeing my distress, switched to 'could do' mode ('we could do this, you could do that').

  She observed my face drop more and my body slump further, and immediately asked 'what do you need from me right now?' She responded straight away to my answer of 'tell me that it's all crap and give me a hug,' by doing just what I had asked. This helped enormously. The next day over breakfast, I was ready for the 'could do' conversation. A helpful response demands the right timing as well as the best process.

- Don't take over. I can't emphasise this enough. People did amazing things for us and I appreciated them and am so very grateful— especially since most of them checked first. They included me in their ideas and went ahead and instigated them when they had my permission. My conversation with Sue-Ellen prior to the appearance of the signs, notices and record book went something like this:

Me—'We're falling apart, it's all a mess.'

Sue-Ellen—'What can I do?'

Me—'We need systems and processes; I'm not sure how or what, but none of our left hands have any idea where our right hands are, let alone what they are doing.'

Sue-Ellen—'What if I do something to help people to help? Joan, we need to give people permission.'

Me—'Go for it.'

I didn't discuss or 'approve' what she did before she put the plan into action, but she afforded me the respect to involve me in what we were trying to achieve with the strategy.

• Those of you who have read the story will know that Philip's last Christmas was horrendous. We struggled as a family to celebrate Christmas. Philip cognisance was sporadic at best and the thought of Christmas decorations and all the celebration that they implied actually made me feel ill.

When a tree (albeit small but nonetheless not invited) suddenly appeared in our lounge room I was horrified—not because it was there, but because I had been completely omitted from any decision to have it. It was one of the first things that got thrown out when Philip died, because it didn't represent Christmas to me—it represented having my needs and feelings completely over-ridden.

This probably sounds completely unreasonable, but at a time when the most important aspects of your life feel completely out of control, it's important to feel some modicum of control over the little things. The person who brought the Christmas tree into the house was undoubtedly trying to be helpful and to do something nice. They would be horrified at how I felt and I don't wish to criticise the generosity of the intention behind the act, just to point out the importance of checking first. Please be mindful of what you do and how far you go. Carers are invariably exhausted and frequently cranky, but they are still people with thoughts, feelings and expectations.

- Beware the trap of becoming the infallible clairvoyant. I know terms like 'I just know he'll be ok' are meant to help, but for some people they push big buttons. Maybe try something more along the lines of, 'this must be so frightening for you both; I'm here to support you'. Of course, another alternative is to just be silent. We don't always have to say anything; being there can be all the other person needs.

Being there after it's all over

In the editing process of this book I received some feedback that the story seemed to stop a little too suddenly at the point of Philip's death. I considered this feedback very carefully. When Philip died the household went from feeling totally out of control and chaotic to an immediate and complete halt. Whereas days had been filled to overflowing with tasks, demands and requirements, suddenly there was nothing. I wanted to represent the shock of this transition.

Again, friends rallied for me. A roster system was set up to ensure, if I wanted it, there was someone available to be with me all the time. I took this support with both hands for the first week. Once the funeral was over I started to have time in the house alone. These were short periods at first which gradually built to whole days and then a series of days. For some months I was regularly reminded that there were people available to be with me if I needed them.

People who had lived through similar experiences lamented to me how, after the person they were caring for had died, people quickly returned to their own lives. As a final suggestion, I would like to say, if you are close to a carer whose role ends due to the death of the person they are caring for, then please remember that a whole new (and often very difficult) journey has just begun for the carer. Again, there is no perfect solution. Regular check ins are helpful and maybe having a group of people who are able to spend time with the person, if required, would be useful.

In the aftermath of death, particularly where caring at home has been offered, the 'caring for the carer' role can be ongoing for some time.

Grief on its own is debilitating and excruciatingly painful. When you add the overwhelming exhaustion that is the result of a twenty four hour, seven day a week caring role, it can take some time for the person to be back on their feet. This is a personal journey and will differ in time and intensity for different people. Knowing that I had people around to help was a great comfort for me.

In whatever capacity, and for whatever reason, you have come to this book I hope *Who Cares* has helped you and provided some ideas and support.

My aim in writing this book was to write the book I wanted to read when Philip's cancer was first diagnosed.

When he announced, quite adamantly, that he wanted to die at home I said 'yes' without hesitation. I was terrified and my fear was justified.

I consider myself to be a capable person with a host of resources. A main component of my work is to help people develop strategies to better manage their lives and maximise their potential. Every resource I had access to was stretched almost to breaking point through the four and half years of Philip's illness.

I don't think it has to be like that. I hope I have been able to offer some help for you and I wish you well on this most scary and challenging of journeys. To hold the hand of someone as they make the transition to death is a privilege as monumental as the one we feel when we hear the cry of a brand new arrival. Having experienced both, I can say that it is also considerably more difficult.

I wish you peace, hope and love.

Joan

Philip 1953 - 2007. A man who made the 'dash' between the dates truly count.

Author

Photograph by Amie Forbes - Eye to Eye

Joan Wilson-Jones is a successful communication consultant and lifestyle coach. Her eclectic (traditional and holistic) approach helps people to enhance their lives. Joan and her partner live north of Brisbane, Australia. They raise horses, donkeys, alpacas, cattle and chickens with help from three dogs. *Who Cares* is Joan's first book.

Joan's communication and lifestyle consultancy is JwJ Consulting. For more information and to see Joan's regular blogs and articles go to www.jwjconsulting.com

Printed in the United States
By Bookmasters